DATE DUE			

Helping Your Child Discover Faith

Delia Touchton Halverson

Judson Press ® Valley Forge

HELPING YOUR CHILD DISCOVER FAITH

Unless otherwise indicated, the Scripture quotations in this publication are from the Revised Standard Version of the Bible copyrighted 1946, 1952 © 1971, 1973 by the Division of Christian Education of the National Council of the Churches of Christ in the U.S.A., and used by permission.

Other versions of the Bible quoted in this book are:

Good News Bible (TEV)—Old Testament: Copyright © American Bible Society 1976; New Testament: Copyright © American Bible Society 1966, 1971, 1976.

The New English Bible (NEB). Copyright © The Delegates of the Oxford University Press and The Syndics of the Cambridge University Press 1961, 1970.

Library of Congress Cataloging in Publication Data

Halverson, Delia Touchton.
  Helping your child discover faith.

  Bibliography: p.
  Includes index.
  1. Christian education of children. 2. Children—
Religious life. I. Title.
BV1475.2.H335   649'.7   82-15380
ISBN 0-8170-0957-4   AACR2

The name JUDSON PRESS is registered as a trademark in the U.S. Patent Office. Printed in the U.S.A.†

Dedicated to

my family

with whom I have grown
in my Christian faith
and to

Carrie Lou Goddard

who first opened my eyes
to a child's concept of God
at
Scarritt College for Christian Workers
Nashville, Tennessee

*For we are partners working together for God
(1 Corinthians 3:9a, TEV).*

Preface

This book has grown out of classes and seminars I have led with parents as they searched for methods and tools for sharing their own faith with their children. All too often we feel that our belief in God, our "theology," can be shared verbally only after formal seminary training. As parents open up to a new understanding of their Christian ministry to children, parents realize that they can share God in simple, everyday words and actions and in spontaneous situations.

In preparing this manual, I have not set down a curriculum for your child's study. Formal curriculum is available through your church and is a very important part of your child's religious training. But rather I offer you, the parent, knowledge of what Christian concepts children can grasp at various ages, and I lift up opportunities that you may use to point out God each day. Our faith is not found only in churches and the halls of seminaries; we experience God every day of our lives. We need only to be ready for these opportunities for worship.

My husband and I have discovered that as we have tried to show God to our children, our own relationship with God has grown. Every time we think through a simple interpretation of our belief and set it into an everyday context with a child, we have brought God into the ordinary. We have become "like children" (see Matthew 18:3).

So enjoy God with your child every day, both in common places and in places where you least expect to find God. We need only to grasp the opportunity and give children the joy of our religion.

Contents

1
Who, Me?

We teach our children every day of our lives. We teach them intentionally or unintentionally. Either we teach them that our religion is important to us or we teach them that we don't place enough importance in our religion to share it personally with them.

You, as a parent, will be the adult to whom your child will be closest before his or her adult years. To share your faith with your child is an opportunity for Christian ministry that cannot be equaled elsewhere. The home is the most important influence in the child's life. We do not aim for a parroting type of learning, but we aim to help the child develop a close relationship with God that will follow him or her throughout life. When asked, "How did you first learn about God?" we want the child to be startled, to have difficulty remembering the exact time and place of personal realization of God. We want God to be such a close friend to the child that the question is unanswerable.

As the child matures, his or her concepts of God will change. They will change naturally because the child changes in growth and development capacities and gradually comprehends some things which were mysteries before. The change will happen smoothly when it takes place on a foundation set by us, as parents, in early years.

Realizing Your Responsibility

To instruct a child is to give the child specific teachings. To nurture is to provide an atmosphere for learning. We instruct while we nurture, and we nurture while we instruct. The two must be

11

linked, or each suffers. Learning cannot take place without a proper atmosphere, and a proper atmosphere prompts learning.

If you have a relationship with a church, you have likely dedicated your child to God in some form of ceremony or baptism. In dedicating your child, you go further than simply following a ritual. You make a promise before God to train the child. Read again the pledge for your child's training that you made to God at the dedication. No matter what the church, an infant dedication or baptism publicly declares the family's responsibility for the religious training of the child, a responsibility undergirded by the church.

Having taken the step of dedicating the child to God we often set aside the thoughts of any religious training, awaiting the time when we believe the child is old enough to understand. Then we feel awkward in approaching the child and rely on the church to fulfill our obligation of sharing the faith.

Just such an attitude kept one mother from even mentioning God in the home. One day, when her daughter lashed back at her reprimand and stormed out of the house, the bewildered mother turned to a friend who was visiting.

"I can't understand what went wrong. We had her baptized when she was small. All through her elementary school years we insisted that she go to Sunday school. And now this. The church just failed to live up to its end of the bargain and teach her right from wrong!"

The woman expected an impossible task in the number of hours her child was at church. Your child will be shortchanged if you depend solely on the church for your child's religious training. Church attendance is no insurance policy against problems.

You may use the formula below to chart your child's educational time. Adjust the hours in parentheses to your child's schedule.

GENERAL EDUCATION		CHURCH EDUCATION	
5 hours × 5 days =	25 class hours	(2)	hours per week
	+ (3) homework hours per week	× 52	weeks
	28 hours per week	104	
	× 40 weeks	− (4)	hours for illness, etc.
	1,120 hours per year	100	hours per year

(3) educational television hours per week
× 52 weeks
156

+ 156 hours per year (educational TV)
1,276 hours total

Is your child shortchanged?

Is God shortchanged?

We have long recognized the importance of general education for our children. During the first years in school teachers help the child to develop working relationships with other children. We expect the school to teach the child to communicate thoughts. We expect the child to learn to read so that he or she can discover what is happening in our world and participate actively in society. We also expect the school to teach the child to handle finances well enough to live independently. We expect the school to equip the child with basic education, enabling access to the job world and development of a career. To do this we allow the school approximately 1,276 hours of the child's life each year.

⇢ In the religious training of a child's life we expect the child not only to develop a better understanding and working relationship with others but also to grow in self-understanding and to develop a value system for actions. We encourage the search for an understanding of why we are here and development of an affirmative direction in life. Above all, we want the child to develop a relationship with God that will serve as a firm foundation for the span of life.

To top this off, we expect the church to teach the child the formal details of our religion—the celebrations and creeds of the church, the heroes and history of the Bible and of our religious heritage, and the application of Christianity to all facets of life.

How is such an undertaking possible in 100 hours a year? Again, your child will be shortchanged if you leave all religious training to the church. Dr. Gordon Thompson, professor at Candler School of Theology, Atlanta, Georgia, stated in a sermon on the family, "The Christian home is the place where you find the meaning in life."

⇢ As you realize your Christian mission of helping your child with her or his religious development, you need take only two major steps. The first is to love your child, and the second is to share your faith with your child. The loving affirms the importance of the child, and the sharing affirms the importance of your faith. With these two affirmations the child can move into the close relationship with God that we covet for our children.

Love and Sharing

A few years ago the popular bumper sticker that read, "Did you hug your child today?" gave some of us a start. All too often we don't see a reason to hug our children, and the children themselves independently pull away from us. We don't know how to look for the "huggable" qualities of our children, and after years of neglect we certainly don't know how to hug the child without feeling foolish.

One of the best ways to find huggable qualities in your child is to look at the child through someone else's eyes. Temporarily ignore any shortcomings. Rather, look at the child as someone you have just met and would like to get to know better.

A physical touch isn't necessary each time you hug your child. Touch is important, but if you have been out of the habit of physical contact, the child will not respond to your efforts at first. You can hug your child with praise, with unexpected favors, and with courtesy. Caring is the primary ingredient in parenthood. One of the biggest cheats a child can ever have is to grow up never knowing what it's like to have someone really care. And a child who has not known care cannot give care easily.

As you love your child, you will naturally want to share your faith with him or her. Who has better opportunity to know your child than you? Usually the parent knows the child better than any other person and can share the faith most effectively.

Yet if hugging is a hang-up with us as parents, then sharing our religious life with our children is even harder. We usually balk, saying that we have had no courses in theology and can't express ourselves. We try to cloister religious expression in the halls of a seminary or believe it hides in the foreign theological terms used by learned theologians.

Bishop Lance Webb in his book *The Art of Personal Prayer* suggests that theology relates to the ordinary. "God is not found primarily in the distant, the terrible, the awesome but also in the near and ordinary, in a baby born into a loving family in the little town of Bethlehem, and in our own hearts."[1]

If a child's father or mother were away for the first three years of the child's life, expecting to return at the end of these three years, how would you tell the child about the missing parent? Would you bring out diplomas and certificates the parent had earned? Would you show the child a book the parent had written or a building the parent had designed? Would you wait until the eve of the parent's return to tell the child about the parent?

You would want to raise the child with a personal knowledge of that parent throughout the three years. You would refer to the parent as often and as intimately as possible. You would say, "Dad would enjoy the sunset we are seeing together," or perhaps, "Mother always enjoys the night when the whole world is quiet and resting from the day." At every opportunity you would remind the child of the parent and help to develop a parent-child relationship even while the parent was away. So it is with God. We want the child to feel close to God even without seeing God.

Our own theology is simply *our belief in God.* We can better understand our own theology by putting this belief into everyday situations with our children on the level that they understand. By applying our religious faith to everyday experiences, we bring out the simple beauty of God's love and of Christ's teachings. We find this beauty in our world, all around us, and through our children's eyes. Then we become, as Jesus taught us, "like children."

Children are not necessarily looking for complicated theological explanations to their questions. In fact, sometimes they don't need any answer at all—they need to be able to share their questioning mind and to know that we are seeking answers to questions with them, side by side. When we are still not sure about our beliefs, it's OK to admit that we are reaching. In that way the child learns that religious development is an ongoing, ever-searching experience and never a closed book. Our relationship with God and our faith in Christ's teachings stand as the foundation of sharing with our children.

Frederick Buechner states,

> . . . faith here is not so much believing this thing or that thing about God as it is hearing a voice that says, "Come unto me." We hear the voice, and then we start to go without really knowing what to believe either about the voice or about ourselves; and yet we go. Faith is standing in the darkness, and a hand is there, and we take it.[2]

So we can share our faith with our children before we have gained full knowledge ourselves.

Realizing this, the next step in sharing your religion with your child is to alert yourself to the opportunities that surround you every day, opportunities for spontaneous sharing with your child. Then, by studying the concepts that a child may grasp at particular stages in his or her life and by understanding the development and relationship of these concepts to one another, you can make use of opportunities that come your way each day.

"I can pray," said my child,
"Anywhere I am,
Even riding on my bike without my hands!"

Little girl, if you believe that
    then you have learned a lesson well,

And God will ride with you
    and walk with you
    and dance with you
    and smile.

There you go—
    spinning cartwheels—
        touching the cool earth with your hands,
        feeling the new grass sprout between your fingers,
        reaching to the heavens with your toes.

There you go—
    with a giggle and a prayer,
    walking with Jesus on a day that isn't Sunday,
        in a place that isn't special,
        in your grubby jeans
        and tangled wind-tossed hair.

Lord, I'm so glad she doesn't need some formal kind of prayer,
For Tammy's learned to talk with you
        while standing on her head,
And Tammy's learned to feel you near
        while doing cartwheels in the air.[3]

2
Experience Now—
Label Later

Michael moved along the candy counter finding each item more exciting than the one he had left behind. A large chocolate rabbit caught his eye, and he moved around the end of the counter and down the other side toward the bunny.

He reached out and tugged the coat beside him. "Mommie, look at the bunny," he said. "He has a big orange carrot!"

As he looked up, the pleasure in Michael's eyes turned to horror and bewilderment. He ran from the strange woman beside him, bumping into brown coats and black coats and scattering packages as he went. Tears spilled down his cheeks as he cried, "Mommie, Mommie, where are you?"

The salesperson stepped out into the aisle and gathered Michael's windmill arms, calmly assuring him that his mother would find him soon.

Through a film of tears the boy looked at the circle of faces above. Each looked down at him, but his mother's face was not among them. Michael's heartbeat pounded in his ears, and he heard the noise of strange voices rising and falling, until he screamed out, "I want my mommie! I want my mommie!"

The people in front of the boy began to move back, and his swimming vision gradually focused on his mother as she rushed toward him. He lunged forward and buried himself in her arms. The knot inside his stomach melted, and the pounding in his ears quieted. He sank into her embracing love and knew he was no longer lost.

Michael was too young to understand Jesus' parables. His ability to reason needed to grow before he could grasp the abstract ideas that the parable of the lost sheep conveys to adults. Yet the young child did experience the concept of a comforting love that soothes the frantic sensation of being lost from your life source. Michael's mother could not *tell* him about the reassuring love of God. The concept of a concerned love had to be encountered. When the boy reaches his teen years and hears of God's comforting love, he will relate it to this experience.

Social Development

A child's development is much like the growth of society. It took thousands of years for society to reach the cooperative levels of today. Yet we expect a child to achieve in a few short years the characteristics that society has taken thousands of years to develop.

In the first two years we expect the child to develop motor skills and to learn the beginnings of elementary social habits. In a matter of months we expect a child to master a language that has evolved over many years, one with which we struggle as adults.

In the third year of the child's climb to maturity we stress additional social standards, standards whose development has spanned the many centuries of our civilization's cultural progress. Through the few years of childhood the child jumps quickly from the independent "meism" of infancy to the small-group living of the family and then into the community, the nation, and the world, and even into a universe-oriented life.

Through a miracle of God the child meets the pace we set for development, demonstrating a gift of growth that many of us adults have lost along the way. But the child depends on help from us as parents, teachers, and friends.

During this growth to adulthood the child moves through several stages of development:

I need.
I want.
I imagine.
I learn.
I understand.

Moving through these stages, the child learns by use of observation, curiosity, identification, cooperative action, educational skills, participation, and conversation.

Faith Development

Authorities on faith tell us that there are four steps in faith development which we all follow. The first is an *experienced faith*. In this stage we act, react, observe, and copy. Interaction with others and opportunities to explore and test are important in this stage.

By the time we reach adolescence we usually move into *affiliated faith*. Belonging, feelings, and authority are important factors in this stage. Opportunities need to be provided for groups where we can share our faith. Expression is important through arts, singing, drama, creative movement, etc. This is the time when we begin to appreciate faith as our story—our way.

The *searching faith* develops during late adolescence and the young adult years. At that time we need opportunities to question and experiment. Critical judgment emerges and we are developing a commitment to our faith, following through with appropriate action.

After moving through the other stages of faith, we may arrive at an *owned faith*. We develop a personal belief of which we are sure, and this allows us to be open to other people's points of view without feeling a threat to our own. At this stage, our belief has integrity; our belief takes action. We have an identity and witness to that belief.

According to Dr. John H. Westerhoff, all persons must grow through these stages. Sometimes we need to be active in several stages, and sometimes we get hung up on one or the other. But earlier stages are the foundation for later developments, and a stage cannot be skipped.[1]

In his more recent book, *Bringing Up Children in the Christian Faith* [see "Suggested Reading," page 125], Westerhoff combines the first two stages of faith as affiliative faith, a faith we receive as a gift from others.

The Building Blocks of Faith

An infant's main concerns are with body comfort and with what is happening in the immediate surroundings. Child development specialists are discovering, however, that infants benefit far more than we realize from our caring concern as we handle them. It is never too early, therefore, to share God with your child. Your baby experiences the concept of God's love through exposure to *your* love. The more love you give to a baby, the more that child is able to give love to others as the years progress.

At whatever age you begin your Christian ministry with your child, his or her development resembles a building process of experiences and concepts. As your child learns that you will supply his or her needs, the child experiences trust that later leads to the concept of reliance on God's laws. Your behavior toward your child lays the foundation of trust and faith that later allows your child to understand and label concepts as his or her religious understanding develops.

Do we withhold food from a child, awaiting a time when the child has full understanding of nutrition and the digestive system? No, nor should we wait until the child reaches the age of theological understanding to introduce the child to God. In a manner of speaking, we back into religion with children. They cannot understand a concept, such as God's redemptive love. We don't try to explain it. However, when the child does something wrong, we can tell the child, "I don't like what you do, but I love you anyway." Then, when the child is introduced to the term "redemptive love," there will be an experience in the memory. The child will understand that God is like a parent, loving anyway, despite disapproval of unpleasant actions.

There are many books on today's market explaining the physical, emotional, and social development of children. A knowledge of developmental concepts would enrich your understanding of your child. In this book, however, as we work with concepts that children develop and then as we relate these concepts to various ages, you should be able to apply the ideas and suggestions to your child. In religious growth, as in any other growth, each child differs, and you must become acquainted with your own child in order to plug into his or her needs.

When my daughter was two years old, I visited my sister, who was a pediatrician. During our stay my daughter developed a fever type of flu. My sister asked whether she normally tossed about in bed upon going to sleep. Suddenly I realized that I did not know my daughter as well as I should. Since she had outgrown her period of occasionally crying herself to sleep, I had tucked her into bed, never aware of whether her early hours of sleep were restless or quiet. We need to familiarize ourselves with our children's spiritual growth as well as their physical growth.

The Habit of Listening

One of the best ways to grasp your children's spiritual growth is to develop a listening habit. You can learn and understand your child's beliefs through listening. Listen to everything. Listen to the excitement of play and the thrill of school. Listen to the problems with friends and the troubles of catching a grasshopper. And listen to the quiet of thoughts; that is, be aware of your child's silence.

Rev. J. F. Sofge, Jr., of First Methodist Church, Jacksonville, Florida, told the story of a young boy whose mother called him to dinner several times and finally went into the living room to back up her spoken word. With impatience she said, "I've called you to dinner five times. Why haven't you come?"

The boy looked up with surprise. "But I only heard you three times," he said.

Then he turned to the orange glow shining through the window and added, "Besides, I'm watching God put the world to bed."

Mr. Sofge said, "I guess it is more important to watch God put the world to bed than to come to dinner."

By "listening to" her son's lack of conversation, this mother learned that God is important to the child, even her young child.

Once you establish the habit of listening to your child, you will pick up any underlying questions. The child will not sit down and expound theologically with you, but his or her spiritual development will become evident during routine conversations if you take time to listen.

In our conversations as parents we too often limit our listening to a tool for discovering what to say next. But we should listen with a real desire to understand the child. If your child sees you only as the person doing all of the talking during a conversation, ready to answer every situation, then he or she will only "sit through the lecture" and never open up and talk.

By listening, you can also discover what motivates your children to thoughts and reflections. What activities most often reveal the deepest thoughts? Let these be innovators for growth. Use them naturally. Dr. Donald B. Rogers in the book *In Praise of Learning* states, ". . . for children, the process of learning about matters of faith is as natural as the process of learning how to talk and how to read and how to live."[2]

Conceptual Development

Children can handle various concepts at different ages. The best rule to follow is to alert yourself to the progress of your child in play and school. As the child develops reading skills, you can begin to encourage reading selected simple verses in the Bible. When science is introduced in school, relate that to God's world and how God planned for us to fit into that world. The study of history offers opportunities to study corresponding eras of church history, and as the child's understanding of our social structures develops, comprehension of God's action through other people begins to break through.

Knowing what is right and what is wrong develops security in the child. As children mature, they are able to understand what is right in specific situations. Their comprehension of justice develops.

Jean Piaget, the Swiss psychologist whose theories on how children learn helped revolutionize modern education, offered a means of understanding the development of a child's comprehension of justice. He told a group of children a story about a boy who comes when called to dinner and, opening a door, accidentally bumps a tray containing fifteen cups, breaking them all. Then he told of another child who breaks one cup while reaching for a jar of jam without permission. When presented with the question of who should be punished more severely, the younger children responded that the child breaking fifteen cups should receive the greater punishment. The older children considered the intention and said that the first child was being obedient in coming to dinner but that the second child was disobedient and should receive the more severe punishment.[3]

Donald L. Griggs, of the Griggs Educational Service, states, "We grow from one 'used-to-think' to another. 'Used-to-thinks' are those things you used to think and don't think anymore. What we need to do, through teaching in the church, is to *encourage the process* of 'used-to-thinking.' "[4]

The Old Testament records the growth of the Judaistic belief in a God of wrath to belief in a loving God. Historically our theology came through a process of "used-to-thinks," just as our children's theology must come. You can understand the "used-to-thinks" of your children and continue to present opportunities for growth. You can say, "Yes, 'I used-to-think' that too," not correcting the idea, but talking with the child and allowing growth. Without confirming a concept which you do not hold yourself, reinforce your children's right to think independently. You might call this approach teaching with commas instead of periods. The commas tell us that there is more to come, that we are still learning.

When your children begin to grow from "used-to-thinks" to new ideas, share your own growth with them. Let them know that you had (or have) some of the same problems they do. You may often feel one way intellectually and another emotionally. You should communicate this to your children. If they know you are a committed Christian and not perfect, then they can identify with you. A Christian is one who is following Christ, not one who *is* a Christ.

Keith Miller shares in his book *The Becomers* the following: "By confessing my humanity *as a committed Christian*, I have joined those with whom Christ lived and came to heal—those who *know* they need a physician (see Mark 2:15-17). And all it cost me was my reputation—*with Christians who have no problems.*"⁵

Just as educational skills are built on previous skills, religious concepts become firm when we lay a foundation of childhood experience. Consider the various conversations you can share with your child over an apple snack.

With the nursery age child you can talk about God's plan for food. Explain that God planned for parents to give us apples. Enjoy the sweet flavor of the apple and the crunching sound as you bite into the crisp fruit. Then very simply pray with your child, "Thank you, God, for the sweet apple." Or, "Thank you, God, for your plan for parents to give children apples."

The kindergartner's experience widens as he or she learns of helpers outside the home and becomes aware of the growth of plants. With the child of kindergarten age you can discuss God's plan for food. God helps the seeds to grow into apple trees, and the farmers grow apples for those of us who don't have apple trees. Then the trucker brings the apples from the farm to the grocery store, and the grocer sells them to us. Each person is a helper and a part of God's plan for our food. An appropriate sentence to add to a prayer at this age would be, "Thank you, God, for your plan for food and for the helpers who work with your plan."

As a child begins elementary school, scientific understanding expands. The child is able to remember previous years, and there is an appreciation of the returning seasons. Therefore, you can introduce the concept of the cycle of seasons as a part of God's plan. Enjoy remembering spring and fall, blossoms and apples. The child can begin to grasp the idea that God helps all things to grow, even children. Thank God for the beauty of blossoms each spring and the excitement of bins of bright, red apples in the fall. Thank God for the growth of everyone in your family since last fall.

By the time children reach middle elementary grades, they begin to understand basic cause-and-effect concepts. Discuss what happens if we eat too much of any food or what happens if we don't eat the proper foods that contain needed vitamins and minerals. Most middle elementary children realize that God's laws are reliable. We will have spring and fall every year. We will become ill if we don't eat the proper foods and will become ill or overweight if we eat too much of any food. Help your child face the fact that we must learn to live within God's natural laws.

These examples may cause you to fear that your child will rebel at what seems a bombardment of religion. I don't suggest that you use every apple snack to discuss God with your child but rather that you be alert to the opportunities throughout your day. Whether it is a snack or a conversation at bedtime, a cut on the foot or a bubble bath, a bulb sprout in the spring or a pile of dry leaves in the fall—the opportunities are all around you. Grasp them and use them to minister to your children. Don't let them slip through your fingers.

The Chinese philosopher Confucius said that a little child going confidently down the road after you have shown him the way is the most beautiful sight in the world. In 2 Timothy 1:1-14 we read about Timothy's heritage in his mother and his grandmother. In his family he had a firm foundation for his adult spiritual growth. His family life prepared the soil for the Christian life that influenced the world for centuries after his death.

No matter what the ages of your children, there are opportunities every day for them to experience the faith. Later on the experience may be labeled with theological terms when your children have more understanding.

In the following chapters we will deal with the child's concepts. You will find suggestions for both opportunities that are spontaneous and situations you may create to help your children deepen their relationship with God. I have included an occasional Bible reference in each chapter. However, you will find most of the suggested Bible references in the chart on page 120.

3

God Created Me—
God Doesn't Make Junk

". . . . from the beginning of time, God chose
you . . ." (2 Thessalonians 2:13, NEB).

Paul Johnson, who with his wife, Kathie Lee, has brought
Christianity to many through song, recalled, "I was raised in a
very conservative . . . evangelical home, . . . but I didn't understand until I was a kid in high school that you could have intimacy
with God."[1]

Our ultimate aim in working with our children is that they will live
in such a close relationship with God that as they mature they will
turn their lives over to God's direction. We want every child to
move toward an affirmative understanding of his or her role in life,
with God the hub of that role.

However, as Paul Tournier suggests, a child must develop and
have knowledge of his or her independent self before he or she can
commit it to God.[2] If children understand that God planned for
them and that God considers them important, then with pride they
can face the world and you may say:

> And God will ride with you
> and walk with you
> and dance with you
> and smile.
> . . . on a day that isn't Sunday,
> in a place that isn't special,
> in your grubby jeans
> and tangled wind-tossed hair.[3]

In this chapter and the four that follow I want to share with you
some of the child's concepts of God's plan for life, the world, the
family, friends and helpers, and death. From these chapters you can

discover both opportunities that are available in our everyday life and how to create situations which will help your child deepen a relationship with God.

A young child cannot understand abstract concepts. In fact, it is not until children reach the later elementary years, and sometimes even beyond, that they begin to grasp the meaning behind our abstract terms.

Juanita missed her uncle when all the family gathered at her grandparents' house. In answer to her question, her parents told her that Uncle John was in the hospital, where the doctors had performed open heart surgery.

Throughout the day Juanita sat apart from her cousins, questions running through her mind. At dinnertime she did not come to the table, and her mother found her in deep thought, staring out the window. When asked what was troubling her, the girl said, "If the doctor had to cut Uncle John's heart open, then maybe God got out. He always told me that God was in his heart. I don't want Uncle John to be without God."

To the child the heart is only an organ of the body. All of the abstract connotations we adults attach to the heart escape the young child's understanding. Later, when Juanita's mind has developed so that she can appreciate abstract thought, she will relate the heart to love, caring, and forgiveness.

Until the time of comprehension, each facet of the child's life acts as a foundation for faith. You, as the parent, stand in the ideal spot for ministering to your child's religious growth.

My Body

Once your child begins moving about and experiencing articles in the home, relate God to the child's body and to growth.

It is never too early to share the excitement over the physical senses with your child. Enjoying soft textures such as cotton balls, fuzzy blankets and sweaters, and even the child's skin or hair can be a time to thank God for the gift of touch. Say to the child, "God planned it that way." The sandbox becomes a learning experience when you speak of the fun we have feeling the sand under our feet and between our fingers. God planned for our feeling.

Opportunities abound for you to share the wonder of God's gifts of the other senses with your child. Tasting cool water on a hot day, hot chocolate after a romp in the snow, and sweet apples in the fall can set the stage for a conversation about God's gift of taste.

There are pleasant smells and not-so-pleasant smells. Without our sense of smell we would miss out on some of the excitement of life. Our sense of smell tells us of many things before we even see them. It's all a part of God's plan.

On a summer night we enjoy the chirping songs of the crickets, and the crackle of the fire on cold winter nights delights our ears. Through our ears a wide world of music awaits. God's creation of the tiny instruments in what we call the inner ear brings delight to us every day.

Not a day passes but that you can share with your child God's gift of sight. Take time to stop and marvel over the intricacy of a new fern, or the excitement of watching the rush of a touchdown play in football. Thank God for the gift of sight.

Your child's bath and preparation for bed can be a time to bring God into the picture. Speak of how the warm bath water makes us feel good all over. And when we rinse the soap off, our bodies feel squeaky clean. God planned for us to have clean bodies. Bath time is also a good opportunity to talk with your child about the body. (Chapter 5, on families, discusses birth and sex.) From the beginning help your child appreciate the body and realize that we are made according to God's plan. The young child can learn that God made parts of our bodies for specific functions: the legs to walk, the arms to lift or to hug, the mouth to eat, the teeth to chew. If you discuss the functions of the body naturally, then when your child learns about sex, the information will fit in as a part of God's plan.

As the child gets older and can understand cause and effect (during early or middle elementary years), brushing teeth and eating the proper foods become tools in learning about God's laws and dependability. If we don't care for ourselves and eat the foods necessary to keep our bodies strong, then we will become ill. Stress that God planned for us to understand our bodies and to eat the proper foods. If we don't get enough sleep, we are grouchy and sometimes get sick. God's laws are steady, and we can depend on them. God is dependable, and we can carry out God's purpose by working with these laws. The justice of God is a part of God's love.

When there is an illness, you, as a parent, may bring out the love of God in your care for the child. Children's experiences of your concern and love when they hurt help them relate to God's love.

As you care for young children (preschool or kindergarten age), tell them about the man who lived long ago, named Jesus, who cared about those who were sick. In simple language share one of the stories about Jesus, who was concerned when people were sick. Use the story of Jairus's daughter (Mark 5:22-24; 35-43) and the Roman centurion's boy, or slave (Luke 7:1-10). (For an understanding of why we speak of "Jesus who lived long ago" to young children, see page 84.)

Speak with your young child about our God who makes hurts better. God planned that as soon as we wash the dirt away from the hurt, it begins to heal itself. Sometimes, if the hurt is too big, we go to the doctor whom God uses to help with the healing.

When children grow in their understanding of the healing process, share with them God's plan for our bodies to begin to heal immediately. Explain that God provides for the antibodies which fight the germs that enter the cut. God also planned for our cells to make new cells to replace the part that is cut. The scab forms on the outside of the new cells to protect them until they are complete. Then the scab falls away when it is no longer needed. The whole process is a part of God's plan.

Point out that when you hurt your foot, the hurt is not in your hand, and when your stomach hurts, the hurt doesn't go into your foot, too. God gave us feeling in each part of our bodies so that we don't hurt all over each time.

When the child is old enough and asks why some people die from hurts and illnesses, you can say that sometimes the hurts or diseases are so bad that no matter how much our bodies work to heal themselves, the "building-up" forces cannot keep up with the "breaking-down" forces. This usually happens only when we are very old or not very strong (see chapter 7). At all times, however, share with your child the understanding that God intends that our bodies should be strong and healthy and repair themselves.

Each development of children brings opportunity to speak of God's plan for growth. When they step on the bathroom scales or stand under a ruler, talk about how God planned for them to grow each year.

With the accomplishments of block stacking and ball catching, your child may learn that God is happy with the new skills just as Mommie and Daddy are happy. Your pride in simple accomplishments sets the stage for your child's future pride in following God's plan for life.

Sports keep our bodies physically fit. Place importance on improvement of the child's individual accomplishment rather than on competition. "You certainly improved the form of your back stroke this week." Or, "That pass you threw at the beginning of the game was better than the one last week. God expects us to work to improve ourselves."

Children may learn of God's plan for achievement even if they are not interested in sports. Any craft or skill that they undertake shows a marked improvement with practice, whether it be knitting, hammering a nail, or playing a piano.

Birthdays mark times to consider God's plan for many kinds of growth. Each year you can remember with your children the progress over the last year. Ask them: "What can you do this year that you couldn't do at your last birthday?" Thank God with them for all they have learned in the past year. God gave the growth (1 Corinthians 3:6b).

Process extra photos of your children and begin albums that record their growth. While enjoying the album during the year, you can talk about how they are following God's plan for growth. When they are adults, they will appreciate the record of early years.

Grandparents are important to young children. They function as persons who have acquired wisdom. If no grandparents are close by, perhaps you can "borrow" some from time to time in order to offer your children experiences with various ages of people. Through relationship with grandparents children can begin to understand God's plan for their own growth from childhood to adulthood. When his or her grandfather pulls your child in a wagon, you can comment, "Grandpa used to pull me around in the wagon when I was little, too. Yes, all people were little boys or little girls before they grew up. It's all a part of God's plan."

Myself

From the very beginning of your child's life, from the first time you hold the infant, you may speak of God and of God's love, whether verbally or physically. Small children respond to physical closeness. When begun early, your gentle handling offers the child an experience of caring and loving that can be understood even before words can be.

Each time you answer your infant's physical needs, adding to it quiet words of assurance and physical tenderness, you are establishing a trust that will later be related to God's trust. You are dependable, and through contact with the dependability of parents, the child easily accepts and understands the dependability of God.

As your children develop, they need to be able to rely on your dependable love even when they have feelings that confuse and frustrate them. With your love sustaining them, they can grow to realize that feelings are neither right nor wrong. They just *are*. Many situations in family life bring out the old problem of feelings versus actions. You can help your children understand that sometimes we have no control over our feelings, but we can learn to control our actions. Children's inner feelings are important and are not to be ignored. Acknowledge feelings, but help children know that God can help us with our actions.

God made us with feelings. Jesus told us to love one another, but sometimes the child feels, "I hate my brother!" Help children to sort out what it is about the brother that they hate. Usually you can single out some of the things that the brother does that the child does not like. It may be because the brother is a little baby who requires much of the mother's time. Acknowledge that what is disliked are actions. Then discover, with your child, some of the parts of the brother that are likable.

Even Jesus became angry (Matthew 21:12-13; 23:13-36). Louis Cassels in his book *The Real Jesus* quotes Professor John Knox as saying that "no account of Jesus could be even approximately correct which did not call attention to his frequent and sudden anger."[4] Jesus was angry, but he did not physically take it out on others. He used his anger constructively (Mark 3:5).

Help your child to realize that it's OK to be angry but that anger and revenge (or "turning against") are different (Ephesians 4:26). Anger is better expressed in words than in deeds.

Training a child to be a "perfect angel" can cause continued disappointment in self later. Children need to realize that it's OK to have angry thoughts and not feel guilty for the thoughts. We need to acknowledge them and if there is an occasional slip, God forgives us and loves us anyway. But the more we know about God—and the more we love God—then the more God can help us to avoid the slips.

When the anger is over, be certain to make use of the natural opportunity to experience the quiet peace of God. Sharing the peace of the calm that comes after anger helps children relate to the quiet peace we speak of in God. Young children may not draw strength from the story of Jesus calming the waves of the sea, but they can experience that quiet peace with you, the parent. The biblical story will speak to them at a later time.

The redemptive love of God is taught when you express your love for your children even when they do wrong. Ignoring the child and showing dislike when there is bad behavior sets a pattern for belief that God takes his love from us when we do wrong. You can firmly show a dislike for the action and administer punishment while continuing to show *love* for the child. Tell your child, "I don't like what you did, but I will always love you. And God loves you too."

Mrs. Brooks Hall of Weston, West Virginia, shared an experience in a church school classroom.

> After a class field trip which was cut short because of misbehavior, I announced the following Sunday in class that all future trips were cancelled. Their silence was broken by a little girl's gentle voice: "If God can forgive us and give us a second chance, why can't a Sunday School teacher try to do the same?"[5]

As a child's failures to live up to expectations mount up and the child has no way to get rid of them, she or he begins to believe that no one—neither the child's parents nor God—can love her or him. At a time of failure a child needs reassurance of our love and of God's.

It is only through our actions, as adults, that our children learn that God is sorry when we fail but still loves us. When we are truly sorry God forgives us. Because God forgives us, we forgive others. Every day we can teach our children to have confidence in God's forgiveness. It is important to keep the unwelcomed act separated in our minds from the child, the child who grows in the love of God. At times, when the child's actions do not reach the standards we set, we love with a sad heart. Other times we love with a glad heart. But always, as Christian parents, we love. A child learns about the concept of God's grace through experiencing *our* unconditional love. Grace is an unqualified, undeserved love. We receive grace without earning it

Rachael, the young daughter of a seminary couple, spent her first year attending classes and chapel with her parents. She was baptized in the seminary chapel, with the support of all of the seminarians. She was loved and accepted unconditionally by the student body. She had done nothing to merit their adoption. The ongoing ministry to her from the students came with no strings attached. They loved her, whether she cooed or cried, because she was a part of the Christian community. Rachael had unconditional grace.

When her parents were graduated, the child was hardly old enough to speak the word "grace" let alone understand the concept.

Yet the Christian warmth of the seminarians' caring concern to a baby unable to justify that love will always be a part of Rachael's relationship with God. With her parents' help she can move easily into an experience of the grace of God.

As children grow older, they not only learn of God's grace when they do wrong, but they also can come to realize that God expects us to learn and grow with our mistakes.

As I opened my front door one day, a young neighbor girl stood on my porch. In one hand she held three tulips, the bottom stems ragged and the tops drooping in three directions. Apprehensively she looked over her shoulder. Her mother gave a smile of encouragement from the street, and she turned to look up at me.

"I'm sorry that I picked your flowers," she said, pushing the red blooms toward me.

I stooped to look into her eyes as I took the tulips. "Oh, dear," I said. "Now the other neighbors can't enjoy the tulips as they walk by the house."

"I won't pick them again," she said. "There are still a few flowers left. Maybe they can enjoy those."

I agreed and added, "Next year the tulips will bloom again, and then we can enjoy all of the flowers."

"Yes," she said. "I won't pick them next year."

As she was leaving, I told her that tulips only bloom one time every year but that some of the flowers in my yard bloom many times and should be picked. I suggested she come back later in the summer and together we could pick some flowers that she could share with her mother.

The girl's mistake taught her a moral value. Such an experience can be used in a positive way, helping a child to learn that God's undergirding love is with us at all times, even when we make mistakes. God can help us through our problems.

When does a child realize that we learn through our mistakes and failures? Some children never learn; therefore, they never admit making mistakes, even as adults. By teaching children that we learn from our mistakes, you teach them to use all parts of life—even the failures—creatively.

It may be many years before the child will fully appreciate the heritage of Jesus' disciple, Peter. It was to the disciple who betrayed him three times that Jesus gave the responsibility of building his church. Jesus understood that Peter had learned from his mistakes. If children have opportunities to realize that we can learn something positive from all our situations, then they will enjoy an assurance of self and a relationship with God akin to Peter's.

The best way you can help your child face mistakes is to offer empathy. No person is without mistakes, and if children realize that we all slip now and then, they learn to admit a mistake and move forward. All things work together for good for those who love God (Romans 8:28). It's as simple as that. There is no need to use involved theological terms, no need to wrestle with ideas which we ourselves have trouble comprehending.

My World

As children feel secure with themselves, they move out into the world with confidence, yet with responsibility for others. There are many ways you can help your children develop the attitude toward others that Jesus taught.

At as early a time as the child can make small decisions, provide opportunities for choice. You might put three shirts on the bed in the morning and ask, "Which of these shirts would you like to wear today?" These early opportunities for experimenting in choice help the child realize that God made each of us a person who can decide. Later, when the child is faced with decisions about how to act, you can say, "God planned for you to learn to use your deciding in the best way for everyone."

Sports are so much a part of our current society that they are begun early in a child's life, often in the earliest elementary years. The original purpose of organized sports for the child was to develop a sense of fair play. Speak often of God's desire for us to treat one another fairly.

As your children's world broadens through contact with other children and adults outside the family, your children begin to notice that people are all different. By conversation and by providing opportunities for children to get to know a variety of people, you can help your children realize that people look different and have different functions in life, but we are all loved by God and cared for by God. You can tell the child, "The Bible tells us that we all have different gifts from God. We each have abilities and talents that God put into us when God made us, and it takes everyone's abilities to make a better world" (see Romans 12:6). Help children realize that we are all individuals, that no one is like anyone else.

In order to become individuals, however, children need to get to know themselves. A time apart is important to children, no matter what their age. It is only through periods of drawing apart and living with the self that the child can cultivate the close relationship with God that we as adults cherish. Be alert to your child's need for solitude and respect it.

With the development of self children work out their own acceptance or rejection of our mores, and sometimes life appears, to the child, to have a double standard. On the one hand, we say that Jesus taught us to love one another, and then on the other hand, when four-year-old Johnny tells us, between sobs, that six-year-old Bob took his toy away from him, we offer our usual reply, "Nobody likes a tattletale."

Actually Johnny is only reporting an injustice to the authority he knows—the adult at hand. Telling Johnny often enough, "Nobody likes a tattletale," tells him that we don't care to become involved. Yet Jesus taught that even becoming involved with the problems of the hated tax collectors and prostitutes was an act approved by God.

There will always be the chronic tattletale, the child who looks for stories to "tell" in order to gain attention from adults. This child has a deeper problem, a need for large doses of adult attention. Satisfying that need with other methods of attention usually breaks the habit.

We must, however, change our response to the child reporting injustices. Johnny's social conscience is very new and confusing to him. He sees Bob's action as a break in the rules he knows. He needs a reassuring adult's words, "I'm sorry that Bob isn't playing according to the rules. Perhaps he needs my help so that he can learn. Children sometimes need reminding when they act in ways that hurt others. I'll remind you, too, if you forget."

With this handling of the situation Johnny will realize that reporting an injustice is a way of helping others remember rather than a method of getting them into trouble. Even if a stern punishment is in order, we should not punish in such a manner that the child reporting the injustice can perceive it as a reward for his tattling.

A boy was suspected of starting a fire in a vacant lot. An adult reported seeing the boy walk through the lot a few minutes earlier, lighting a cigarette. When approached, he denied it, and his brother stood by the story. Later his parent commented, "We have been very strict about teaching our children not to tattle on each other. I wouldn't have admitted it either."

There are times for tattling, and there are situations not important enough for tattling. A good rule to follow in reporting injustices might be whether the injustice damages the person, property, or selfhood of the other person. Your attitude about involvement speaks to your child, telling of your understanding of Jesus' words, "For I was hungry, and you gave me food. I was thirsty, and you gave me drink. I was lonely, and you made me welcome" (see Matthew 25:35).

Become alert to your own children's needs and problems. Be aware of their hurts, emotional ones as well as physical ones, and express your concern. Then they will learn altruism. Speak often of the hurts of others. By alerting your child to the problems of other people, you are setting down a foundation for the understanding of Jesus' story of the good Samaritan. As you speak with your child about someone who is hurt, you can "remember a story that Jesus told about a man who helped." The Jew-Samaritan relationship in the story is beyond the young children's grasp, but they can appreciate the fact that someone did stop to help the man after others passed him by.

Many of our television shows today portray shooting and hurting. Usually the story centers on the excitement of the marksman hitting his mark and then moves on, leaving the person who was shot where he fell. You can help to develop compassion in your child both by bringing out the fact that the person who was hit is in pain and by playing down the emphasis on the marksmanship. The time to stress marksmanship is during target practice with a legitimate target, for example, when preparing for hunting animals. (See page 50 for reference to hunting.)

Any time that you experience something pleasant, you can say, "God loves us and gave us good things. Because God loves us, God expects us to love and expects us to share with others." When your child acts in a loving and helpful way, observe, "We show our love for God by the way we act." It is important that you relate good actions as expressions of love for God, instead of actions in fear of God's punishment. Stress the thought that we are good because we love God, not because we are afraid that if we are *not* good God will punish us.

As Donald Rogers said, "Children listen. They do not listen for a systematic theology. They do not listen for a complete recital of biblical history. They listen for the occurrence of God language in reference to the problems of their lives. Does God relate to their fears? Is God seen as concerned about their problems? Is God dependable?"[6]

When I was a child, my parents gave me assurance that I could establish any career that I wanted and come out on top. They added the phrase "through Christ," for they truly believed that our strength came through Christ. But I was too stubborn to add Christ's help to my strength. The modern emphasis on the independence of the individual sometimes puts the stress of Paul's words at the beginning of the sentence instead of the end. "*I* can do all things in him who strengthens me" (Philippians 4:13, italics added).

I thank God that my parents also helped me to develop the foundation of a relationship with God that grew. Through that growth I realize now that my strength comes from God, not from any independent ability of my own. Together God and I can accomplish the needs of each day; together we can establish my position in life and move through a meaningful career. The relationship becomes a partnership—not an asking-receiving relationship, but a junior-senior partnership where I, as the junior, am open to the guidance and leadership of the Senior Partner.

God even understands my struggling over a career direction, because he experienced indecision when Jesus spent time in the wilderness wrestling over a choice between dramatically proving his divine sonship by throwing himself down from the temple and quietly working through the lives of friends and followers. God can relate to my problems from a human experience.

How much service we can bring to our children if we establish a faith relationship early so that they bring God into all of their lives! Then it is natural in the planning of a career, in the choice of a mate, or in everyday situations that God be a part of their decisions.

Paul states in his letter to Thessalonica, ". . . from the beginning of time God chose you . . ." (2 Thessalonians 2:13, NEB). To be chosen is important to children. A part of children's growth depends on their belief in self and acceptance by others. As part of a family and a Christian community, your child can begin to relate to the posters that state, "I'm OK, because God don't make no junk!"

4

God Planned
for the World

All things bright and beautiful,
All creatures great and small,
All things wise and wonderful:
The Lord God made them all.

Each little flower that opens,
Each little bird that sings,
He made their glowing colors,
He made their tiny wings.

The purple-headed mountain,
The river running by,
The sunset, and the morning
That brightens up the sky;

The cold wind in the winter,
The pleasant summer sun,
The ripe fruits in the garden:
He made them everyone.

He gave us eyes to see them,
And lips that we might tell
How great is God Almighty,
Who made all things well.[1]

Throughout the annals of Christian tradition we find references to the wonder of God. Our Judaic heritage, in the Old Testament particularly, speaks of humanity's amazement with God's creation. Today in our churches we raise our voices in hymns of wonder and praise to God. The heritage is rich, and we want our children to experience the awe of God's greatness. But how do we pass this heritage on to them?

A child is naturally curious and observes the surrounding world. But this interest can easily diminish if we, as parents, do not reactivate our own senses and become a part of the child's wondering mind. During our growth to adulthood, as myriad activities clamor for our attention, we often develop a blind eye and a deaf ear to the obvious, everyday world.

Do we spend more time discussing the mysteries of math and of science than we do God? Do we forget that God is the source of those very mysteries? Do we stress nature as a laboratory of science, or do we see it as the work of God, and men and women as scientists struggling toward a deeper understanding of God?

It is important for you, as a parent, to watch for occasions to see God in nature with your children. Provide opportunities that will prompt them to questions. When children ask the questions themselves, they are more interested in the answers.

In this chapter on God's world I hope that you will find tools and discover times when you can share the creative and dependable facets of God with your child. The natural world in both urban and rural communities is the most accessible opportunity one can use to develop a relationship with God.

Vera Holmes baby-sits as many as six children in her home regularly. To each child her mother-substitute name is "Not-Mama." Most of the parents leave for work very early in the morning, and as the children arrive at her home, they gather around the breakfast table in front of an east window.

One morning during breakfast their view of the world suddenly changed from darkness to an enveloping pink hue. The fog of the warming earth reflected the colors of the rising sun, bouncing pink off buildings and tipping each leaf and blade of grass with its own glow.

One of the boys looked up from his cereal bowl and asked with wonder, "Not-Mama, why is everything pink outside?"

Vera put her arm around the boy's shoulders and silently shared the beauty with him for a moment. "It is beautiful, isn't it?" she said. "You know, we have a big day today, and God gave us a pink morning to begin it!"

The child would never have understood the scientific reason for the sun's reflection in the air. Yet Vera helped the boy to grasp an understanding even beyond any scientific reason: God created it that way.

Iris V. Cully in her book *Christian Child Development*, speaking of children under seven, states that the "why" that they ask requires only a casual explanation, one to which they can relate. When they ask, "Why does a tree have leaves?" they do not want an answer involving roots and sunshine but rather an answer that relates to the world they know, such as "to give us shade."[2] We may add, "God planned for the shade to cool us when we are hot."

Patty walked out the door with her mother as a neighbor left their apartment. The adults talked leisurely while Patty stood nearby. Suddenly the girl noticed a caterpillar on the sidewalk. During a break in the conversation, Patty called her mother's attention to her discovery. The mother mechanically answered, "Yes, that's nice," and launched her adult conversation into another subject.

The next Sunday at church school, Patty told her teacher about the caterpillar. The teacher told the girl that a caterpillar is a part of God's world, a part that changes. She said, "Just like you were a baby once, and are changing and will be a woman, the caterpillar will someday become a butterfly. God planned that babies become men and women and caterpillars become butterflies."

The teacher was wise to relate God and the divine plan to Patty's interest in the caterpillar, but how much more effective it would have been for the development of Patty's wonder over God and the world if her mother had taken two minutes to stoop down with the girl and marvel over the insect right then! The mother and the neighbor would have also strengthened their day with a brief experience of worship.

Children learn best through here-and-now experiences. All of the "remember whens" that a teacher can put into a session can never take the place of a "here and now."

Harley Swiggum, founder and director of Adult Christian Education Institute (headquarters for the Bethel Bible Study), said, "One hour in the living room with the parent talking about Christian concepts is worth six years in Sunday school in terms of effectiveness."[3] I would just add to his statement, "One hour in the living room or *any* other place." The effectiveness of the child's learning is the here and now, not the then and remembered. And you, as a parent, naturally have the most here-and-now opportunities available.

Stop on the sidewalk, with trucks and cars rushing past just a few feet away, and marvel over the grasses growing in the crack in the sidewalk or between the sidewalk and building. Watch for a tree that has grown close enough to a sidewalk to push the cement aside. God's plan for growth continues when the necessary water, sunshine, and minerals are present.

Sometimes we panic about verbally sharing God's creation with our children because of varying views on the creation story. If your ultimate desire with your child is to develop a close relationship with God, then the particulars of the creation are not as important as the experience with the Creator. Remember that ". . . faith here is not so much believing this thing or that thing about God as it is hearing a voice that says, 'Come unto me.' "[4]

During the preschool years a child best learns about God's creation by associating God with beautiful things. The simple awe of the beauty around him or her reaches a climax as an awe of God. The heavy frost on a playground fence becomes a worship experience with a preschooler when we bring God into the picture. Stop and marvel over the tiny ice crystals, and share God's gift of frost with your child.

As children grow in scientific knowledge, then the awe of God, who made it all and conceived such a plan, becomes even greater. Children grow from "used-to-thinks" to new ideas naturally.

When your children are old enough to realize that God works in our world not only through routine procedures but also through change, they can appreciate God's plan for changes such as the progressive growth of a forest. In what follows I summarize the progression; you can observe stages of the progression all around if you are aware of the process.

When a yard or any piece of land is left dormant for a period of years, a plant succession transforms the area from open space to deep evergreen woods and finally to a mature grove of hardwoods. In the first stage of the process you will notice various seed-producing grasses and weeds. The field mice and rabbits tunnel through the clover and grasses, and, if the property is in a rural area, deer graze there, too. Birds foraging for grass seed drop additional seeds and berries and new species appear. Soon there are thistle, wild astor, sorrel, plantain, blackberry, and pokeweed. In two to three years the broom sedge often crowds out the other weeds. This thins the ground cover, producing the ideal condition for pine seeds to germinate.

Within a few years the pine seedlings appear above the remaining forage, and an evergreen forest has begun. In about ten years the pines dominate the area, reaching about fifteen feet in height. They shade the ground and deposit a mat of pine needles, making the soil too acid for most other plants. For several years the pines dominate the area, and the red squirrels, jays, warblers, and nuthatches thrive.

As the pines mature, they lose their lower limbs, competing for the light. The understory is now open for hardwoods. Since pine seedlings require sunlight, they offer no competition for the maple, gum, and poplar seedlings which do well in the shade. The seeds of these hardwoods are brought in by the wind. In this forest small animals begin to browse and build their homes.

The pines naturally thin themselves, being susceptible to disease. The rotting pines attract insects and fungi, and soon the woodpeckers move into the forest. As the pines fall, they join the rotting leaves on the ground to become the "sacrifice layer" of soil (humus). The pine, leaves, insects, etc., give up life to form a rich soil. This is God's plan to recycle a stump.

Forty years after the first pine seedlings, the hardwood forest is on its way, with trees large enough to show a blaze of fall color under the pines.

About sixty years after it all began, the forest stands thick with hardwoods, several pines looming above the canopy of branches, like sentinels standing watch. The early hardwoods (maple, gum, and poplar) dominate the growing generation of oaks and hickories that were planted almost totally by squirrels.

The hundred-year-old forest has seen a succession from weeds to pines, then the hardwoods seeded by the wind or planted by squirrels. As the sentinel pines die off, there is an understory of dogwood, redbud, and other smaller trees indigenous of the area. Short woody plants and low, shade-loving shrubs develop, and a mature forest begins to reproduce itself each fall, by dropping its seeds into the decaying matter beneath.

And so, watching for vacant land can be an opportunity to observe the continuing creativity of God. Help your child spot the varying stages of God's active creation. The weedy field or deserted yard may be spotted as the first stage. Look for small evergreens peeping above the weeds and guess the length of time God's re-creation process has been at work. Then find the dense pine forest, and you have located the next stage. With a little practice you can guess the age of the hardwood forest by spotting a sentinel pine above the canopy.

And at every opportunity marvel with your child that God,

recreating in a dependable fashion, works through change in our natural world.

God not only planned for the changing re-creation in nature, but he also planned for a continuing growth of trees, no matter what the circumstances. Some pines, such as the northern jack pine and southern pond and sand pines, produce tight cones which do not open under normal circumstances. The cones remain tight, protecting the seeds inside, until they have been exposed to excessive heat. God planned that when a fire rages through the forest, destroying all the trees and all the seeds on the ground, these pine seeds will remain protected in the cone. After the heat of the fire is gone, the cones open naturally to release the beginnings of a new forest. It is all a part of God's great plan for re-creation, and we share such a wise and omnipotent God with our children as they begin to discover the marvels of God's world.

The older elementary child has worked with science enough to question some of the areas that are still mysteries to humankind. As your children question, you can tell them that we (civilization) are learning more about God's world every day. We are learning how to control diseases and how to capture the power of the sun and the wind. We are learning the patterns and causes and effects of weather so that we can better predict storms and take precautions. All of this knowledge is a part of God's world, and God gave us minds to work with the knowledge. Working with science to develop a better world is working with God.

No matter what the age of your child, you can begin to share our obligation for Christian stewardship of God's creation. The very young child can understand that we help God by caring for plants that we place in our house and around the yard. As the children grow older, they can understand that conservation of paper and fuel are methods of Christian stewardship for our natural products.

The dependability of God is obvious all around us. At sunrise or sunset share with your child that God planned for the sun to rise every morning, and we can depend on God. Marvel over the reflection of the setting sun on a building. God made the night for rest and the day for work. Night is our gift from God.

As your child understands that our seasons come in a cycle, share the return of the seasons as a part of the dependability of God. God planned that the seasons would happen in a particular way every year. When the leaves fall, new leaves will take their place next spring. The birds fly south in the fall and return each spring. Even if the cold of winter seems to go on forever, the buds of the dogwood will open every year. It has happened in the past, and we can depend on God's plan for it to happen this year too.

Ray Stevens's record "Everything Is Beautiful" can be enjoyed at the change of seasons. Ecclesiastes 3:11a tells us that God "has made everything beautiful in its time."

Spring

One of the most exciting times to share God and nature with your young children is during the springtime. The cold and rain or snow during the winter has kept them indoors. Their memory of previous springs, especially before the elementary grades, is not keen, and the freedom of the out-of-doors comes upon them with a fresh newness. Enjoy searching for God's little surprises in the flower bed and among the grasses. Daffodils and tulips seem to sprout up overnight, and the tiny violets hide under the leaves before they open up to the world. Look for new tufts of grass in the cracks of the sidewalk.

A meaningful springtime tradition that has been a part of our family for twenty years is waxing onions. Paraffin, or old candle wax, along with pieces of crayon to give additional color may be melted in cans placed in simmering water. A sprouted onion is dipped in the melted wax several times, allowing the onion to cool briefly in between. Additional color can be spangled over the colored onion by touching a hot knife to the ends of crayons, allowing the melting crayon to drip over the waxed onion.

We find that a basket of brightly colored onions brings the joy of springtime indoors. By placing the onions away from the hot sun or from a direct source of heat, they will last for weeks, continuing to sprout new life after a dreary winter.

The young child (up to the early elementary years) enjoys the array of colored onions and the experience of creating beauty. When your child is old enough to understand abstract ideas, the sprout's growth from a seemingly dead bulb can be related to Christ's resurrection. (See pages 93-96 for a discussion of Easter.)

When the onion begins to wilt, cut the sprout off for salad and break the wax away from the bulb. Plant it outdoors and it will grow another bulb. Help your child to realize that stewardship of our food and care for our earth are part of God's plan.

You may want to begin the anticipation of spring a little early with your child. A branch with a blossom or leaf buds, full but not yet open, will burst forth sooner when brought into the warm house. If you place it in water on the table, each day's growth becomes a worship experience as you marvel over God's creation and dependability.

Enjoy the new baby animals that abound in the springtime. Visit the zoo and count the number of baby animals. As you drive through the country, point out the calves and lambs. In your neighborhood, perhaps even among your own pets, you will have the opportunity to enjoy kittens and puppies with your children. Speak of how God planned for animals to have animal parents to care for them just as human parents care for children.

As the birds return, hang a net bag full of strings and hair for the birds to pull out and use to build their nests. If you are fortunate to be the host yard for a family of birds, observe the parent birds sharing in nest building and feeding.

In many areas March brings gusty winds. You might ask your child, "Did you ever think that God is very much like the wind?" One of the earliest questions a child asks about God is "Where is God?" Share with your child that we cannot see God with our eyes, but we can know that God is here. The way we know God is much like the way we identify the wind. We cannot see the wind, but we can hear the sound as it blows through the leaves. We can see what the wind *does*. We see it blow the seeds in the air and push the blades of a pinwheel. We can feel the coolness of the wind on a hot day. God is there even if we don't see God. We see what God's power does, and knowing that the power is there makes us feel better.

The older elementary child, when learning about Pentecost, can understand how Luke spoke of the coming of the Holy Spirit as like "the rush of a mighty wind" (Acts 2:2). Wind is air, and we cannot live without air, just as we cannot live without God. The wind is like God's power. God's power is here, and we know it is here. We feel the effect on us, but we cannot see it.

Listen for the sounds of God's spring. When it rains, remind the child to listen for the drip of the water from the eaves at night while he or she is lying in bed or the splash of a puddle when your car drives through it. Stop and listen to the sounds of spring.

In the city as well as the rural areas you can help your child notice signs of spring. Parents begin taking babies for strolls and the ice-cream vendors appear on the street. You might say to your child, "Look, the flower man is on the corner again. That means that spring is here, just like last year. God is dependable; God brings the warmer weather and the springtime every year."

Whether you live in the city, a small town, or the country, you can help your child experience God's plan for new life by observing sprouting seeds. You may plant the seeds either in a small plot of ground outside that the child will care for or in pots indoors. Or place seeds on a wet blotter between glass pieces so that you can watch the sprouting process. Marvel with the young child over the ability of a small seed to sprout roots and stem. Talk with older elementary children about the plan for seeds to give up protein, starch, and mineral matter to form new life. They will begin to grasp the concept of Christ giving his life for us. Remember that the experiences of the young child build a foundation for later understanding of spiritual concepts, such as our salvation through Christ. Even without the child's understanding the concept of Christ's sacrifice, the joy of springtime is a real experience.

One of the greatest revelations of God's power with a single seed came to me one day as I helped to load and unload trailer-loads of wood from a large oak my husband had cut. At first I basked in the anticipation of the warmth of winter fires. Then I began looking at the stacks of wood and marveling in a new way over the growth of an oak. And it all came from one small acorn—because God planned it that way.

Renew your faith with your child during the spring season. View the world with eyes and ears open to evidences of God's plan, and rejoice in words and in song. Many of our hymns of joy speak of the evidence of God in springtime.

> Let all the world in every corner sing:
> My God and King!
> The heavens are not too high,
> His praise may thither fly;
> The earth is not too low,
> His praises there may grow.
> Let all the world in every corner sing:
> My God and King![5]

Summer

"This is the day which the Lord has made; let us rejoice and be glad in it" (Psalm 118:24).

Summertime abounds with opportunities to share God's world with your child. You can speak of how the weather is warm to help things grow. Enjoy a fountain or stream and the cool shade God gave us. Work together with plants, marveling over their added growth each day. Talk about God's plan for food. Discuss how some food consists of the roots of plants, some of the leaves or the fruit, and some of the seed of plants. Use a trip to the grocery to discuss this aspect of food, or visit cornfields, orchards, and groves.

In the morning notice together mushrooms that have sprung up overnight. Talk about how some things grow quickly and others, like the giant oak, take years to grow. There are olive trees in the land where Jesus lived that were alive 2,000 years ago when he enjoyed their shade with his friends. Giant sequoia trees in California, between 3,000 and 4,000 years old, are among the oldest living things on this earth; yet some plants live only a day. God has a plan for growth for everything on the earth, and each grows according to that plan.

Stop and marvel over the tiny insects; enjoy the intricacy of their design. Talk about the ants, how they busily gather food for the winter. Enjoy the industrious squirrel, hiding nuts for the coming season. Watch the spider spin its web. Share with your child the spider's persistence and dedication to the web's design. Perhaps you may find a web that sparkles with droplets of dew. As you speak of the design and symmetry of the web as part of God's creation, begin to look for other designs and shapes in creation. Some shapes are symmetrical, and some are asymmetrical (or free form). Look at shells, flowers, corn, ladybugs, crabs, apples, acorns, and people.

Appreciate with your child the beauty of a bowl of fruit or flowers. Talk about how God made beautiful flowers and gave us color. God didn't have to make them colorful; God could have made the whole world black and white. Thank God for the colors and for letting us see the colors.

Enjoy the textures of God's world. Even a creeping child can enjoy the textures of rocks, sand, and grass. Speak of the difference between textures of the dog's fur and the feathers of a bird. Some textures are smooth yet bumpy, such as an ear of corn. The honeycomb has a rough texture, and yet it is soft. When you are fishing, invite your child to feel the different texture of various fish—some have scales, and some have skin. In your explanation of textures make use of a magnifying glass. Textures and shapes and colors are all God's tools in creating our world.

Listen to the quiet noises. The rain sewer makes a different sound from the water that plops from the trees after the rain. Seek out the sounds of running water, too. Sometimes the water slips along the ground with almost no noise, and at other times it seems to sing joyously.

Listen to the bird calls. Each has a different type of voice, and some of the birds have varying calls depending upon their current needs. Stop and enjoy the rhythm of the drumming woodpecker and the soft whistle of the pigeon's wings. When you hear a rustle in the leaves, investigate the lizard or beetle industriously searching for food.

Take a night hike; pick out a noise and track down its source. Our senses of hearing and smell sharpen at night. Without the distractions of daytime noises, we can listen more easily. Crickets, frogs, and a host of insects fill the nights with sound. Or you might want to get up some morning at daybreak and concentrate on morning sounds. By listening closely, you can hear the hum of insects and the occasional snap of a twig as a small animal searches for breakfast. You may hear a busy squirrel running across the roof of the house, excited over another day of gathering nuts.

Enjoy the clap of thunder and marvel over the fireworks of the lightning. Talk about the different shapes of storm clouds. Tell your children that sometimes we don't understand the destruction caused by a storm, and often the noise is frightening, but we know that we can trust God even during a storm. If they have learned the scientific reasons for storms, marvel over the mysteries of God's creation. After the storm is over, enjoy the rainbow together should one appear. Thank God for letting us see the colors. When your child is old enough to grasp God's promise in the rainbow, share your appreciation of God's covenant with Noah. Then the next morning remember that you watched God wash the world the day before.

Talk about lakes and rivers and God's plan for our use of them. They provide us with transportation and electric power as well as with water to drink and fish to eat. Talk about the ecology of the river with your older elementary child. It's all a part of God's overall plan that, for instance, the amount of rain and the watershed conditions in the upper river valleys affect the condition of the oysters where the river empties into the bay. If the rain did not wash down to the bay the nutrients of decayed leaves from trees high up in the mountains, the oysters in the oyster beds would die. We must learn of the interwoven parts of our world in order to work with God.

When you find a tree that has been cut down, count the rings. Talk about the process of growth, how the tree puts on additional growth each year according to God's plan.

With your child, blow on a dandelion and talk about the different plans God made for transportation of seeds. Maple and elm seeds also travel by wind. Throw some up into the air and worship God as you watch them float to the ground. Many grass seeds are moved about on animals' coats or our clothes. When your dog comes into the house with a burr in his tail, talk to your child about the seed. Squirrels and birds move many seeds from place to place. Notice tiny plants that grow around a fence or wall where a bird enjoyed holly berries or chokecherries. People often move seeds about as they eat various fruits and vegetables.

If your family uses a compost pile for your kitchen scraps, by late summer you may be able to dig up miniature citrus trees, an example of how people move seeds about. One year we had a break in our sewer line, and the next summer a crop of tomatoes sprouted up around last year's repair! Even the modern convenience of a garbage disposal had transported seeds! Everything works together according to God's plan.

Going to the pool, ocean, or lake is a favorite pastime during the summer. With your child thank God for cool water when we are hot. It is also important to discuss God's gift of our minds which help us understand that we must not go into deep water until we can swim well, or that we need to learn about the undertow of the ocean and respect it. God also expects us to know that too much sun produces severe sunburns so that at times we need to protect ourselves from the sun.

Your older elementary child can see God's creation in the pattern of the tides and begin an appreciation of God's universe by learning the relationship of the moon to the tides.

When we purchase ice cream today in a cardboard box or a plastic pail instead of making it ourselves, we lose an important opportunity to observe God's plan. If you have a chance to make your own ice cream, tell your child what the ingredients are. Talk about the cream from the cows and how it is a part of God's plan for us to depend upon animals—and for them to depend on us. Share God's plan with your child when you prepare other foods with animal products.

By the time children reach older elementary age they may understand the general pattern of ecosystems. My father's favorite example of God's plan for the world to work together was the effect that the number of "old maids" in England had on its navy in years past. He told me that years ago most "old maids" in England owned cats. The cats ran through the fields and feasted on mice. The more cats there were, the less mice, and this was helpful because the mice ate the clover in the fields. The fewer mice to eat the clover, then the better the clover, and the cows grazing in the field had better food. With better food the cows produced more nutritious beef. And because of the better beef for the sailors, England had a stronger navy. We all must rely upon one another in God's plan.

Enjoy an evening under the stars. Gauge your child's ability to appreciate the parts of God's universe by his or her scientific exposure. A child of any age can look up at the stars and remember that Jesus enjoyed the same stars with his parents many years ago. The stars are so universal in time and place that they act as ties to our heritage.

Every observation with your child can become a spontaneous worship experience. Worship is not a set form in a building called a church. Worship is deepening your relationship with God, whether it is talking about your child's love for a puppy or marveling over the reflection of the sun on windows. Thank God at any time for the world. Sing the doxology with your child when you enjoy a part of God's world that usually goes unnoticed. Praise God, from whom all blessings flow!

Autumn

Autumn is the season in which change is most obvious. Often it comes upon us suddenly.

If your child is a kindergartner or older, you may want to begin a book which would record the signs of God's seasons. Purchase one of the hardbound, lined ledgers or make up your own book. Your child will look for signs for you to record in the book. Illustrate the book with drawings—and don't forget the title page with the name of the author! We all take pride in our work when it bears our name.

Begin early looking for and recording the "signs of fall." Days become shorter, and the temperature cools. Study your record of the sun and temperature, and observe God's pattern of shorter days and colder nights as the season passes.

In many areas colorful leaves are the most obvious signs of fall. Enjoy the blaze of color with your child. Spend time walking in the leaves and listening to them crunch underfoot. Make leaf raking a celebration. Your job may take longer, because children get caught up in the thrill of watching the leaves float through the air, but your children will relate to God's change of seasons best by participation. Throw leaves into the air, and make autumn a worship experience.

Record the migration of birds as they leave your area or pass through on their way south. Some of the larger birds are very noisy in flight. Each year at about the same time a flock of grackles move into the woods behind our house. They make their way down the hill and across the creek, moving as an army across the dead leaves. I can stand outside and hear their progress as they rustle the leaves, searching for small insects. Then I know that fall is upon us, and God's year of seasons has come full cycle.

A young friend was visiting me this fall, and we were picking the last fruits of the garden. Suddenly we were conscious of thumping noises in the natural area nearby. Upon investigation we discovered a squirrel sitting atop the nearby pine, breaking off the young cones and dropping them to the ground. He stopped briefly when we moved closer, and then resumed the activity with even greater speed. Later, when we returned to the spot, all of the cones had been removed from sight, stored away for the winter.

As you observe squirrels collecting acorns and burying them, talk with your child about God's plan for each tree to produce enough acorns to feed the squirrels and for squirrels to bury more acorns than they will use during the winter so that some will sprout and make new trees. Acorns are God's promise for spring. God wouldn't make them if there was to be no spring. Be sure to bring leaves, cones, and nuts indoors. As you arrange them in vases and bowls, speak of God's creation.

One of the obvious signs of fall is what some call the "October blue sky." Thank God for the variety of shades for every color. The sky displays a range of color, the shade depending upon the weather and the season.

During the fall many families enjoy hunting trips. If your family goes hunting, take advantage of the opportunity to observe God at work in the changing world. Talk about how, many years ago, the animals that provided all the meat that people ate had to be hunted in the woods. Now we breed animals specifically for food, but we also hunt some of the animals that we enjoy eating. A young child (before middle elementary years) will have difficulty understanding the dependency we have on the meat of animals, but as children grow older they begin to see the world as a whole. The attitude you have toward game hunting will help children appreciate it as a means of acquiring food. Tell them that God wants us to kill only what we can eat. We must be certain to leave enough animals so that they can reproduce themselves.

In most of our country the harvest time and our official Thanksgiving holiday are weeks apart. Growing up in Florida, I never knew the true feeling of a harvest time. It seemed to me, from my subtropic experience, that Thanksgiving was a date arbitrarily set. Harvest occurred year round. In fact, the height of the picking season came in early June, and by mid-July the gardens gave up and were replanted in the fall. When I lived in the north, I found a true harvest experience. I pickled, canned, and froze every tidbit that our laboring plot of ground produced. I even suffered the thorns of wild buffalo berry bushes for their translucent red-pink berries. At the end of all the work and turmoil, I truly felt thankful. But then I waited a full six weeks for our traditional Thanksgiving dinner.

Perhaps we should consider a special dinner of thanks at the time of our harvest. Children relate to God's gifts from the earth more easily if they have helped to pull the carrots that very morning. Nothing says that we must have only one thanksgiving dinner each year. Thank God with a special celebration when you can see the results of your creativity with God.

Use the time before the traditional Thanksgiving dinner to build an appreciation for the fact that all people give thanks across our country on one special day. Talk about God's plan for food. Point out that we work with what God has provided by storing it so that we can enjoy it later. Let the child experience freezing and canning as a way of working with God.

Build a Thanksgiving mobile from pictures in an old seed catalog. At obvious points around the house, post pictures of growing foods and of families eating the food.

Act out harvest time to the tune of "The Farmer in the Dell."

"The farmer . . . plows the ground . . . plants the corn. . . . The seed grows in the ground. . . . The rain falls on the ground. . . . God makes the sun to shine. . . . God makes the seed to grow," and finally, "What a wonderful God we have, Hi, ho, the derry-o, what a wonderful God we have."[6]

One of our familiar hymns, "Come, Ye Thankful People Come," can be used in preparation of the season because it speaks of the gathering of people and the processing of grain. In many families Thanksgiving is a time for reunions. The hymn can be sung at mealtimes throughout the fall, anticipating the time when we will be together with aunts and uncles and cousins. As you prepare food, use the hymn as an expression of joy. Many verses in the Bible, particularly in Psalms, are appropriate for the harvest. Check the chart "The Child/the Concept" for helps.

Winter

Our general outlook on winter is usually one of dreariness. Yet if we think about God's overall plan for the world, we can find many spontaneous opportunities to share God with our children during the winter.

After the glorious array of leaf colors in the fall, the bare limbs of the hardwoods seem bleak. Help your child to understand why God planned for the trees to lose their leaves in the winter. I was an adult with elementary age children of my own before I fully appreciated God's plan for bare limbs in the winter. I had learned of the scientific dormancy of trees, and I knew that evergreens went through a dormant period even though they did not drop their needles. However, I did not relate the two types of trees to their capacity to shed snow.

One fall a severe winter storm hit early, before our trees had shed their leaves. The wet snow broke a branch of our young basswood tree. During previous winters many feet of snow had fallen and blown around the tree, at times almost covering it. But only three or four inches of early snow, before the leaves fell from the tree, broke the branch.

Share with your child God's plan for trees with spreading limbs and leaves that do not shed snow easily to lose their leaves each fall. Notice the evergreens during the snow. In the area of the country where heavy snows fall they are shaped in such a manner that the limbs droop, causing the snow to slide easily to the ground. Other evergreens have needles that are thin enough to allow the snow to move through them so that snow does not accumulate and put stress on the branches. God has made everything according to a plan.

With today's soaring energy costs our children certainly will hear us discuss fuel bills. Share the warmth of the sun with children. Encourage them to play in front of windows where the sun shines and provides solar heat. Point out that the bare limbs of the trees allow the sun to reach in and warm us, and thank God for the plan for trees to lose their leaves in the winter and for the sun to warm us. Appreciate new designs of houses that make use of earth and snow for insulation and sunshine for heat.

Older elementary children can begin to understand that oil and coal are fuels that God stored underground during past centuries. Now we use the fuel to heat our homes and to run our automobiles. Children can also realize that God has many plans that we have yet to discover. God has plans for solar and wind power, plans for understanding the weather, plans for overcoming diseases. We work with God in discovering the plans and putting them to use.

Earlier in this chapter we thought about the symmetrical patterns found in nature. During the winter take special note of individual snowflakes, an example of radial symmetry. Enjoy studying each design with a magnifying glass. Notice that all snowflakes have six lines, or points, and each line or point from the center is identical. Yet no two snowflakes are alike. God planned infinite variety in these icy crystals.

Walking on freshly fallen snow gives us a feeling of walking in a new world. As you walk on new snow, suggest to your child that we might imagine what it was like when the first people walked on God's earth. Enjoy the pattern of footprints in the snow, and thank God for the fresh snow.

Sometimes when you awake on a winter morning, you can sense that snow has fallen in the night, even before you look out the window. Help your child to listen for the stillness that comes over the world when snow falls without wind. Listen for the crunch of tires as the first cars move out into the streets.

As the weather gets colder, notice the fur thickening on your pets and your neighbors' pets. Children will appreciate God's care when you tell them that the thick fur is God's way of preparing the animals for winter. God gave us minds to know how to protect ourselves from the cold and gave the animals a thicker fur coat every winter. Talk about God's plan to help animals live when times are difficult. God planned for some animals to go into a hibernation period and gave them an instinct to build their houses with natural insulation. Preschool children will appreciate God's plan for the animals, and as they mature, you can talk about ways that God helps us, too, when times are difficult.

Help children realize that we can help God by caring for our pets. Domesticated animals have become dependent upon people for help. By taking care of the needs of a pet, your child can experience a partnership relationship with God in caring.

When our daughter was young, she decided to trim our cat's whiskers. We had not thought to talk about God's plan for cat whiskers. When we told her that cats enjoy going into tight places, where they may get caught, and that God made the whiskers of each cat to grow to the size of the spaces their bodies would fit into, then she moved into a more caring role with our cat. We assured her that God also planned for the whiskers to grow again should something happen to them, and she watched over the cat until the growing process was completed.

A bird feeder outside a winter window sets the stage for many conversations about God. By recording the different birds which come to the feeder, you can detect the migration patterns of some birds. You will find that certain birds stay in your yard year round. Talk about the way that God cares for birds. God provides enough grass seed both for the birds and for the grass to reseed itself. God planned that birds should fly south, away from the areas where snow covers their food supply of seed and bugs. When we put up a feeder, some birds that would normally fly south will stay; so once we begin feeding the birds in the winter, we must continue. In addition to a feeder, you might like to make suet balls and hang them for the birds, or attach a string, or wire to a pine cone and spread peanut butter between the cone's scales.

On a cold, dreary day in the winter take a walk outside and talk about God's dependability of seasons. The world is cold and nothing grows during the winter, but new life is hidden under the snow. Search for seeds hidden away that are waiting for the warm spring weather. Check the bare limbs of the trees. Some of them have buds that formed during the summer, buds that are waiting for the warmer days when they will burst with leaf and flower. We know that the bare limb will bloom in the spring. It has done so every year, and it will happen for many years to come. That is God's plan, and God is dependable.

5
God Planned for Families

"That was a good cake you made, Mom. It's my favorite!" Paul carefully cleaned up the last crumb from his plate.

His mother smiled as she took the dish to the sink. "Thank you, Paul. I knew that you liked coconut. I especially made it because I love you."

By speaking openly of your love as it relates to your caring, providing, and being concerned over the hurts of your children, you help to relate words about love to the experience of love. Then when you speak of God's love, children can connect God's love and care to the happy times they recall when parents said, "I did this because I love you."

Even a very young baby understands the warmth of a cuddling arm when the world seems threatening. Keeping a child close at hand while you work around the house helps to build a family closeness even before the child can understand it. You can easily do this with infant seats and baby slings. A young child feels closer to the parent when the child is sitting in a lower drawer of a kitchen cupboard and playing with the pan lids than when the child remains in an elaborately decorated nursery playing with a toy manufacturer's finest products.

During the past year I met two infants who are wrapped in close love and care daily, although the parents of both infants hold full-time, outside-the-home positions. The job of the mother in one case and the father in the other is such that during most working hours the infant may sleep in a bed in the parent's office or travel about the building in an infant seat. Each morning when the child arrives he receives a wealth of loving from his parent's fellow workers.

God's Love and Family Love

Talk spontaneously with your child about relatives and how they show God's love. After enjoying a greeting card, say, "Grandmother sent you the nice card because she loves you." When an older child helps the young one to dress, grasp the opportunity to say to the younger child, "Sister helped you to dress. She loves you." And say to the older child who helps, "The way that you help care for your little brother is much like the way that God loves and cares for us."

On a cold day, as you wrap a warm scarf around a child's head at the door, make a simple statement of love: "I love you and want you to keep warm." The child will be doubly warm, both from the scarf and from your love within. Your touch, as well as your word, communicates love.

A child relates God's love to the love he or she experiences in the family. In a church school class the children had spent two Sundays thinking and talking about the Lord's Prayer. At the close of the second session the group prayed the prayer together. Afterwards a little boy drew his teacher aside.

"I don't want to pray 'Our Father,' " he said.

Upon the teacher's inquiry he responded, "I will pray 'Our Mother,' but I don't want to pray 'Our Father.' "

During the week the teacher spoke to the minister and learned that the child's father often came home drunk and beat the boy. He could not relate to the first words of the Lord's Prayer because from his father he had not experienced love, only fear. All that had been said in the classroom about the love of God he related to his mother. And so he wanted to pray the prayer with the substitute word. One can be thankful that the child had experienced love from his mother.

As adults, we have an image of a God who, like a parent, is reliable and dependable. We understand that although our human parents sometimes have flaws in their character we can depend on a loving and caring God. The preschool child understands "Father" or "Mother" only as his or her daddy or mother. The child's mind has not matured enough to comprehend the relationship of parenthood that we associate with God. Until that time of understanding, it is better to address your prayers to "God" instead of indicating a more specific parental relationship. Later, after experiences with parental love, the child comes to appreciate God as our parent, our loving God.

Family Time

Every child needs adult time (i.e., time with parents) as well as opportunities to play with other children. Our lives become so crowded with our adult activities that we find it easy to tell our children, "Go and play with your toys (or with other children)." We seldom stop to spend individual time or family time with them. If you tell your child consistently to go and play, you convey the attitude that you want the child to go away, that you don't want to be bothered.

One summer we set up a routine for each child in our family to plan and prepare at least one meal each week. The original purpose for the experience was to teach the children, son and daughter alike, enough about cooking to enable them to be self-sufficient. Yet the great plus of the plan came when parent/child conversations developed. The child responsible planned the meal before I purchased groceries each week, and on the appointed afternoon I assisted while each prepared the meal. I peeled carrots or set the table and was available on the cooking scene for advice. During the preparation time we enjoyed conversations that would never have taken place in our rushed schedules. After that summer I decided that the dishwasher may have been as destructive to the family as any other modern convenience. Washing dishes by hand forced families to spend some time together, and communication between parents and children, or between brothers and sisters, naturally happened. I, personally, prefer to substitute other family times for dishwashing. But we need to be certain that another time is found.

Set aside some time each week for your family to talk together. Begin early in your family life to clear the communication lines between family members. Occasionally you may feel that a family time serves no practical purpose, but as long as such times provide situations for you to talk together or to enjoy an activity as a family, then the communication lines stand open for any crisis that arises.

You might begin your first family time by asking everyone to tell of something special that they like about each person. Talk about special activities during the week, about people to whom you have talked and stories you have read. There are several books offering suggestions for such times. *The Anytime Book for Busy Families* by

Crystal Zinkiewicz (see "Suggested Reading" section) makes a good handbook for developing the communication lines within families. She recommends that you share conversations beneficially when you travel in the car, among other times.

Become more intentional as a family. Recognize and appreciate the family relationship, and plan activities to strengthen the bond. Help children realize that although everything else around them might be in a mess, you are still together as a family, and that fact is important. God planned for family members to support and help one another.

Learning About Families

One of the ways that children may learn of God's plan for families is through experience in play. Encourage children to play through family situations, using dishes, dolls, cars, and blocks. Stop often to talk about the play experiences, asking them to tell you what the make-believe family is doing and how they feel about the activities going on in their make-believe world. Speak often of God's plan for families. You might say, "You are cooking the food for your family, just as I cook for our family. That's why God planned for families—so that we can help one another." When the make-believe parent has punished the child, ask, "How do you suppose the child feels? How do you feel about this as the parent?"

A new baby brother or sister joining the family offers opportunity to discuss God's plan for parents to care for their young children until they can care for themselves. Prepare for the new member of the family ahead of time. Talk about how children grow each year and can do many things they could not do as babies. Speak to each child of how you cared for him or her as a baby. Refer to the specific activities that the children can do now but that the new baby will not be able to do, and how you will have to help the new baby to learn. Ask the children to think of ways that they can help the baby.

Talk about how your family's love is big enough to be shared—not divided, but shared. This lays the foundation for understanding God's all-encompassing love. Young children cannot understand the parallel, but having experienced a shared love, they will later be able to label it as an encompassing love.

Observing animal families can be an occasion to talk with your child about God's plan for families. Animals have families and people have families because baby animals and children need someone to care for them until they can care for themselves. Speak of the fun we have doing things together as families, and thank God for families.

Enjoy activities with other families, and realize how their families are different from yours. Talk about the different types of families in God's plan: families with many children, families with one child, families with two parents, families with one parent, families with grandparents living in the same house, and even families with only one person. You might want to help your child make a book about families with pictures drawn or cut from magazines.

Weddings are busy times, and often the child is caught up in the rush and excitement of the occasion but does not understand the spiritual meaning of a wedding. Talk to your child about the ceremony. At a wedding two people tell the world that they want to be together as a family, loving each other. When Christians marry, they often have the wedding in the church, which is a way of showing that they want God to be part of their life together.

Discussing marriage as a Christian's acknowledgment of God in the family life adds the dimension of God's plan to bearing children. Tell your child that you were so happy together as a family before he or she was born that you wanted to share the happiness with him or her/the child.

One of the best references I have found for sharing sex and childbirth with children is *The Wonderful Story of How You Were Born* by Sidonie Matsner Gruenberg (See "Suggested Reading" section). The book tells the story of how a child is born and grows bigger. It uses the "Do you remember when you were a baby?" approach and then talks about families. There are two "stories" in the book, naturally dividing it into two sections. The first story is for younger children; the latter story, written for the older child, brings more facts about the reproductive process into the story. Although the book does not make specific reference to God, it provides ample opportunity for you to incorporate God naturally. The story is told beautifully and with a natural emphasis on the family; by sharing this book and adding your explanation of God's plan for babies to be born into families, you offer the Christian attitude toward sex and families to your child.

Another important ritual involving the family is the baptism or dedication of a baby. Be certain to include an older child in this ceremony. A further discussion of baptism will be found in the chapter "The Church and Your Child."

Weddings and baptisms offer opportunities to share photographs with your child from your own wedding or the child's own baptism. Such occasions can naturally grow into a discussion of how you, yourself, were a part of another family at one time when you were young. The beginning of your child's pride in Christian heritage develops as you talk about those in your larger family who live today and who lived long ago. We are all part of God's plan.

Family Traditions

Traditions help to weld a family together. Traditions say, "This is *our* family. This is *our* story. This is the way that *we* do it. We are a part of this family because we do it *this* way." Such a confirmation of the child's part in a Christian family helps with the second stage of faith development, that of an affiliated faith. Consider the occasions and activities that you participate in as a family. Begin a list, and from these you can arrive at opportunities to speak with your children about their Christian heritage and about the traditions in your family.

Perhaps you enjoy hiking or canoeing. Say to your child as you hike or canoe, "We enjoy God's world together as a family." Sports may be an important activity for your family. Say, "God planned for you to develop your body and to learn to play fairly with others." Trips are perhaps important in your family. Point out to your children, "As we travel, we find people everywhere who live together as families." Attend churches during your trips. You might say, "There are families all over the world who are Christians."

Your ethnic heritage helps to establish traditions. Our family makes *lefsa* (a flat potato bread) each year, remembering our Norwegian heritage. A Ukrainian family I know makes and exchanges *pysanky*, eggs hand-painted with wax between a series of dyes. There are many traditional meals whose roots reach into family heritages. Enjoy your ethnic heritage as a part of God's plan for families.

Speak with your child about the traditional family occasions that Jesus knew in his family as he grew up. The Seder and Passover celebrations center in the family. On Friday evenings in Jewish homes the family begins the celebration of the sabbath with mother lighting the candles and father blessing the cup of wine.

The Christian holidays offer opportunities for establishing traditions. Plan a workshop time within your family to prepare for Christmas or to consider the meaning of Lent. Decide on the date(s) of this activity in advance and mark it on your calendar so that every member of the family knows of its importance and will schedule activities around it.

Traditions within the family establish a foundation. However, don't try to remake your family overnight. Add bits here and there, fitting new traditions naturally into your present life. Build on existing traditions, establishing a togetherness as a Christian family. A good process is to begin a file of ideas that fit into your life-style. Or you may plan a calendar of ideas that you would like to implement throughout the year.

Encouraging Responsibility

An important part of children's experience of family life is the growth of responsibility. There are many jobs around the house that children can do to develop their sense of responsibility. Caring for younger brothers or sisters develops dependability in the older child. God expects us to care for those younger than we, whether in our family or another family. Speak of how God planned for each person to do his or her part in the world and that in our family we all have jobs to do in order to keep the house and yard in such a condition that we can enjoy living in it.

In order for both of our children to learn to carry out all the jobs around the house our family established the "job jar" routine each Saturday morning. Those jobs to be done were written on slips of paper and put into a jar. The children drew a slip of paper in turn, and the jobs that fell to them were their responsibility that day. We did not allow them to exchange jobs, because we felt it was as important for our daughter to learn how to mow a lawn as it was for our son to clean a toilet. When they grew older, and we knew that each had learned to master all of the arts of housekeeping, we allowed them to agree between themselves on permanent jobs. Consequently, when we must be away from home and leave one or both of the children, we can expect to return to a house as clean as when we left.

Your own actions will communicate to your children God's desire for us to be responsible and dependable. Your routine of planning meals on schedule and establishing regular bedtimes develops your child's trust in you. By providing clothes to wear and seeing that they are ready when needed, you tell your children that you care. If you cannot play with the children one day because of wash that must be finished, tell them that God expects us to carry out certain jobs and that one of yours is to see that the family has clean clothes. After you take care of the clothes, follow up on your promise to spend time together.

Through experiencing a trust in parents, the child moves toward a trust in God. Beginning when the child is quite young, stress the trust we have for one another in a family. Be truthful with your children about leaving them, and upon your return offer assurance of your love. Even as children grow older and become independent, it is important to let the members of the family know where you are going and the approximate time of your return. From the time our children were old enough to read we left notes for them if there was a chance they would return home while we were even as close by as next door or across the street. Because we kept them informed, as they grew older our request that they tell us where they were going was not unrealistic but natural. We stressed the importance we hold for one another, and should an emergency arise, it is only a loving consideration to know where to reach the other person. With this approach knowledge of one another's whereabouts and activity does not take from our independence but rather adds to the caring and trust we feel for all members of the family. The inside of one of our cupboard doors has a variety of often-used notes, and the outside of the door becomes a current bulletin board of messages. If schedules must be changed, or traffic holds us up beyond the expected time, we stop to make a phone call home. The same is expected of our children, and the responsibility becomes an act of loving concern for the other rather than an invasion of privacy.

Once trust is established between you and your children, honor and respect for you as a person will naturally follow. Honor and respect for parents lay a good foundation for respect for God.

6

God Planned for Helpers and Friends

"We are God's fellow-workers" (1 Corinthians 3:9a, NEB).

This verse is a favorite reference for church school curriculum. As a parent, you can make effective use of it at home and in the community as you develop an awareness of God's plan for people who help us.

Your children see you prepare a meal, but are they aware of all the people who helped in one way or another to bring that food to the table? Talk about the clerks at the grocery store who help us to pack the food in the bags when we buy it. Talk about the other employees in the store who place the food on the shelves so that we can see just what we need. When you do your grocery shopping, make a point to drive around behind the store and point out truckers unloading the food. Think of other links in the food chain between the farmer and your table. Speak of them as God's helpers.

Be alert to opportunities for sharing God's helpers with your child. Besides the food chain of helpers, include doctors, teachers, people who work while we sleep, police, garbage collectors, television actors, construction workers—the list is endless. Once you tune your mind to looking for God's helpers, you find them all around you.

Develop a calendar with your children. Call it a "Thanksliving" calendar. On each day write down anyone who has been one of God's helpers that day, someone who has done something kind for your children. Plan opportunities to express appreciation for helpers throughout the year.

Why wait until the church school class studies about helpers for your child to learn to offer thanks for God's co-workers? The teacher may not realize that your child visited a hospital or thrilled over watching a fire truck race down the street. You are closest to your child's experiences, and you are able to point the way toward God and say, "Look, that's one of God's helpers!" Let the excitement of the moment be a part of the learning. Perhaps you just chanced upon turning down a street onto which a fire engine pulled out of the station; by that chance, there's God, and there's *your* chance to hold God's plan up for your child to grasp. Stop and thank God right then for God's helpers, the firefighters.

Recognize every opportunity to point out God, and watch your own faith grow as you share it with your child. By using everyday situations your life and your child's life become celebrations of thanksgiving and thanksliving.

Although the family stands as the important center of the child's faith development, you will find that by broadening their exposure to others, your children will experience new ideas. A neighbor's child returned from play school one day, excited over the "Our Father" that she heard another child talking about on the playground. She wanted her parents to teach her the prayer. My neighbors said that they had not talked with their children about God or prayer and hadn't actively thought about such matters themselves for many years. They had always thought that someday, when the children were older, they would involve them in a church school somewhere. Now, at an early age of four, her child was leading the family into an experience of prayer.

God made us with a need for other people and a need to share ourselves with others. John H. Westerhoff states,

> Our created corporate selfhood places us in an essential relationship with *all* others. Because God is in relationship with all persons, we cannot be in full community with God unless we also identify with and seek the good of *all* persons.[1]

This brings us to the concept of friendship. Friends are important. We cannot live a Christian life without them.

Be alert to opportunities to talk to your child about friendship. Realize that we do not gain friends by some magical experience but that a common interest can develop into a friendship with the help of our own interest and thought. There are joys with friendships, but there are also responsibilities for the proper caring of a friendship.

When children do something that promotes friendship, tell them, "That was a good thing to do for your friend. We share with our friends because we love God, and we love our friends."

Help children plan surprises for a friend. Talk about the friend and what the *friend* would like to receive as a gift. Help children think about how they would feel if they were the friend.

When you learn about a new friend, ask just what it is about that person that your children like. Thank God together for friends. Then ask your children how they can show friendship to another person in the same way.

Children in the elementary grades can understand how our actions prompt responses. Discuss kindnesses to other people that make them happy. When they are happy, then life is happier for us, too. This is a way of working with God's laws for a better world. God planned that making others happy would make us happy. Suggest that the child try an experiment of smiling at people who seem unhappy and count just how many smiles are given in return.

Talk about several friends that your child has and how each is different. Discuss the things that your child enjoys with each friend and how each friendship is also different. Some friendships last for many years, and some, because we change, are short friendships. The authors of an excellent book on friendship, *The Heart of Friendship*, say that "each friendship, like each star, has a life of its own! No two friendships are identical."[2]

Today's world of transfers and life changes places a strain on friendships. Help your children to realize that important friendships will continue, even over the miles. And wherever we go, we can find Christian friends who enjoy the same things we enjoy.

Encourage the development of friends across age, racial, and national lines. As your children become acquainted with older people, speak of the way that God helps us through the friendship of older people. They lived through some of the same problems we face every day. Provide opportunities for visiting people in nursing homes with your children.

When our children were small, an extended care facility of a hospital was within a block of our home. Because of my involvement in the center, our children would often meet me there after school. One of the older men was their favorite person, and as soon as they came in the door and checked in with me, they went straight to the gentleman's room. Sometimes I had to search them out when I was ready to go home. They had found a friend across the span of years.

In some of our cities or suburban areas the opportunities for development of friends from other nationalities and races is limited. Books will help your child realize that although people may look different than we do, they enjoy many of the same things we enjoy and can be our friends. Locate stories of children who are involved in activities that your child particularly likes but who are of a different race or nationality. Sometimes you can arrange for opportunities of interaction between clubs or groups to which your child belongs and other groups with members of a different race or nationality.

During our children's early years we lived in towns with no families of another race, and the towns were so far from other communities that there was no opportunity to develop relationships. When we learned of a program to bring children from the inner city of Chicago to the plains of the Dakotas for two weeks, we volunteered to share our home with a boy. As the visit progressed, we realized that what we were sharing with our children was not so much an experience of relating to a person of a different race as one of sharing our home and our open country with a child who had lived in a totally different environment. Later, when the children had opportunities to develop friendships across racial lines, but with common environment, they realized that color of skin does not make the difference as much as the opportunities for development of the gifts that God has given each of us.

In helping your children experience friendships, talk freely about the individual ingredients in our lives that make up the whole person and how each of us is a separate person; yet we are all loved by God equally.

Amos wrote, "Do two walk together, unless they have made an appointment?" (Amos 3:3). Your children can grow to experience God as a friend, too. God always has an appointment open for us, and we need only to accept it. Through prayer, whether your children are young or older, they can grow in a friendship with God.

7

Death: A Part of God's Plan

Every child, at one time or another, deals verbally or inwardly with the mystery of death. In fact, research indicates that 80 percent of children's fears concern death.[1]

A child comprehends death differently at varying ages. According to a study of 378 children done by Marie Nagy in Hungary, children under five years of age seldom accept death as final. Sometime between five and nine, their concept has advanced enough for them to realize that the person who died will not come back. However, unless they have experienced the death of someone close, they tend to ignore the possibility of death happening to them. A popular idea at this age is that the selection of those to die is strictly by chance. About the time children reach nine or ten, they begin to realize that death is universal and that at some time everyone will die.[2]

As Christian parents, the faith we have to share with our children speaks about death. Often, however, we shy away from sharing this part of our faith because we are unsure of it ourselves.

As with many other concepts of the Christian faith, when we forget about the adult level of understanding and strive to understand as a child, we gain in our own faith. Consider methods and ideas that you can share with your child. Feel free enough to write them down. Before you know it, you will become aware of your own beliefs and experience spiritual growth yourself.

Jo Carr in her book *Touch the Wind* tells of her daughter's simple theology about death which explained many things to her.

Sometimes it will be the child, not the parent, who does the articulating. What you think needs to be said is hard to say. You can't think of the words. It happened like that at our house the night our neighbor died. Mr. Primm, next door, was Julie's daddy, and Martha's—a kindly man who always had a cheery word or smile, even for small neighbors. And now, quite suddenly, Mr. Primm was dead. Becky and Doug lingered at the supper table after the older ones had left. "They are thinking about Mr. Primm," I surmised, "wishing they really understood what it was all about. They are feeling a little of the loneliness that must be almost overwhelming to his own children tonight. Maybe they feel a need to talk about it but don't know how to or whether to bring it up."

I didn't know how to or whether to, either. What can one say about the death of a good man, to a child who is barely six, and another who is almost five? But still they sat there, gazing with unseeing eyes at the pictures on the backs of the cereal boxes.

"Uh—," I began, thinking how eloquently I'd *like* to be able to say it. "Mr. Primm is dead. We are sorry, for Julie and Martha will miss him. We will miss him, too. He was a good neighbor. But there is something for us to remember at times like this—that death is as much a part of life as birth. It is just as natural, just as much a part of God's plan. And God who loved Mr. Primm when he lived next door still loves and cares for him, and still loves and cares for his family."

Becky nodded gravely, her eyes wide with the intuitive wisdom that children sometimes reveal. "I know," she said. "The preacher came to our Sunday school class last Sunday, and we talked about it. He said it's like a cocoon."

Doug looked up with interest. Cocoons he could understand.

Becky went on. "A cocoon looks all dead. In a way it *is* dead, because it is shut off from the world that it used to know. Then one day. . . . " Becky paused, her eyes mirroring the delight of the vision she described. "One day, the cocoon opens up, and a beautiful butterfly comes out." Doug's eyes were bright, too. Butterflies were happy creatures, and he would wish happiness for his friend Mr. Primm.

I hugged Becky close for a moment, partly out of gratitude that she had expressed for me, in terms with which they could both come to grips, that which I had found so hard to say.

But Becky pulled loose. She wasn't through. She said, "You know, that caterpillar in the cocoon didn't know what it was going to be like, to be a butterfly. It didn't know how it would feel to fly. All it knew was that it had to spin that cocoon. So it did it."

She frowned, thinking of the unlovely creature settling down to a task it did not understand. "After it became a butterfly, it remembered what it was like before, but it didn't want to go back."

Oh Lord, God—I should explain the mysteries of life and death to these thy children? The simple trust of their faith explains many things to me.

It was truly a moment of worship. But it would not have happened for us if we had not *tried to put it into words*.[3]

No matter how well we, as children or adults, understand the joy of a Christian concept of death, we cannot sidestep the normal process of grieving. Joyce had grown up in a Christian home and felt confident in her theology about death. She knew that she was fortunate never to have experienced a death among her close family and friends, but she believed that when the time came, she would be able to face death with an outlook of joy. When a neighbor's husband died, Joyce sympathized with her as she grieved, but all the while she prided herself in her own spiritual growth, believing that her neighbor's grief was a lack of faith.

The next summer Joyce's mother developed a cancer which caused extreme suffering before her death. Joyce had been very close to her mother, and the death left a void that her husband and children could not fill.

From all outward appearances Joyce moved through the crisis, drawing strength from her faith in Christ's relief for her mother's pain. But inwardly she experienced a resentment that her mother was no longer nearby. She fought with herself, rereading the Scriptures for assurance. She considered herself a mature Christian; yet she repressed an anger with her mother for dying, with the doctors for not discovering a cure, and with God for allowing cancer to be a part of the world. The feelings were there, but she would not face them and admit her deep grief. As the months passed, Joyce found excuses to stay home on Sundays and avoid her Christian friends. She felt that she had lost her faith.

Joyce did not realize that although her Christian faith was deep and she acknowledged and embraced the belief in life after death, her feelings of grief needed to be worked through. Her faith was not lacking, only her understanding of the normal process of grief.

The story of the death of Lazarus in John 11 tells us that as a human being Jesus experienced grief. From the time that Jesus heard of Lazarus's illness, his intentions were to use the death as a learning situation for his followers by raising Lazarus from the dead. Intentionally he waited two days before going to Bethany. However, when he arrived at Bethany and saw Mary and Martha's grief, he also wept and took the time to share their grief, even though he knew that he would raise Lazarus from the dead. Jesus understood grief from experience and accepted it as a natural process to be worked through, not to be glossed over.

The Stages of Grief

The first stage of grief is a short time of shock. This numbness gets us through the necessities of settling the immediate needs after a death. If the person who died had suffered from an extreme illness, then this stage may begin for family and others before the death.

When the shock wears off, the pain of acute grief sets in for a period. Often this second stage includes restless sleep and a loss of weight because of a lack of appetite. Many people also experience anger or disorganization and withdraw from life.

After working through the pain of the loss, we can begin the third stage—to work to rebuild life. Then we can understand Paul's statement—that everything that happens fits into a pattern for good when we love God.

A child may not understand the stages that grief follows, but we can help the child to understand that our sadness is not so much for the person who died as it is for the fact that we will miss the person very much. Our faith tells us that God has something great planned for us after we die, but our feelings of loneliness are still there, and are natural.

It is important that children receive extra security at the time of a death and feel a part of the family, of the sorrow, and of the supporting love of our Christian community. Let your children see you cry, although there is no need to expose them to hysteria. The routines and rituals of the family should be continued. Performing physical activities will help to release the strain.

The "Really, Really Me"

When John Quincy Adams was eighty, a friend met him on the street and asked how he was that day. Adams brightly replied, "John Quincy Adams is very well, thank you. But the house in which he lives is becoming dilapidated; it is tottering on its foundation. I think John Quincy Adams will have to move out of it before very long. But he, himself, is very well, thank you." [4]

In her book *Helping Children with the Mystery of Death* Elizabeth L. Reed shares a poem written by a nine-year-old girl:

> Where is the really, really me?
> I'm somewhere, I know, but where can that be?
> I'm not my nose, nor my mouth, nor my eye,
> I'm not my feet, nor my leg, nor my thigh.
> I'm not my hand, nor my arm, nor my hip,
> And I'm not my teeth, nor my tongue, nor my lip.

I'm sure I'm not my elbow or knee—
Oh, where am I? Oh, where can I be?[5]

Elizabeth Reed suggests that a game of "Where Is the Really, Really Me?" will help a child to grasp the difference between the death of the body and the living of the "really, really me," the part of us that likes another person, that loves to be cuddled, and that chooses to help someone else.

A child can cope with death more healthily if you have talked together in a natural setting before the stress of the loss. Grasp opportunities for such conversations.

By discussing growth and change, you can help prepare children for death. Ask, "Where is the baby that you used to be? You've changed." Then talk about how they will be even more different as an adult and that the child will no longer be there. Death is yet another change in God's plan.

Stress the parts of the world upon which we can depend. Day always follows night; spring brings buds and flowers after the winter; harvest follows a summer of growth. Thrill over the sunset and sunrise. Enjoy the order of the night sky. The moon becomes a sliver of light and disappears, but we can be sure it will be large in the sky again. Visit a planetarium, or purchase an inexpensive night chart and follow the order of the stars. Enjoy Psalm 19:1-4 together. If you establish God as the dependable force in the changes of nature, then your child will naturally accept God as dependable after death.

As the leaves fall from the trees each year, enjoy the color and crunch underfoot. But also speak of how the buds will come forth in the spring. Show your child the places on the bare limbs that hold the secrets of the new life to come in the spring.

John Quincy Adams's reference to his house growing old and dilapidated brings to mind all sorts of possibilities for conversation starters. A child outgrows clothing, but the clothing is not the child. The hermit crab lives in a shell until it outgrows the shell. Then it moves on and finds a larger shell to use as its home and protection. We outgrow our houses, too.

Enjoy a dewdrop with a magnifying glass. When you touch the dewdrop, it seems to disappear. But actually it is drawn into the atmosphere and changed into vapor. Later, it becomes water again.

The cocoon and butterfly help us to realize that change can be beautiful. Ask your children if they remember what it felt like before they were born. A baby is very happy in the mother's womb, and coming into the outside world must be a scary experience because the baby doesn't know what to expect. Death is much like that for us. We don't know exactly what to expect. But we can always rely on the plan that our loving God has made for us. Our experience of life has shown us that the rest of God's plan is all-wise and all-loving, and so we know that we can depend on God. The part of the person we love is with God after he or she dies, even as we are with God.

There are many other opportunities in nature to discuss death through cycles of change and God's dependability. Refer back to chapter 4 for additional ideas.

The death of a pet can provide an experience to share, although it cannot be compared in degree with the stress of the loss of a close member of the family. Share the sadness about the pet's death with your child. If the question arises about whether the pet went to heaven, say that you don't know but that God has some plan. Don't tell children anything you don't believe or aren't sure of. It's OK to be unsure; emphasize that we trust God. Show that you love the pet and will miss it. Then when people die, the child can see that a person is important and not forgotten since their pet was important.

When our daughter's dog, Jingles, was killed by a car, we immediately purchased a new dog. We told her that we still loved Jingles but that our love was big enough that we could love Jingles and the new dog, too. After studying the process of death, I realized that we should have spent time grieving the first dog's loss before filling our void with the antics of a new puppy. The professionals suggest that such a move might cause the child to fear that love can be turned off easily and that we would immediately seek a replacement should the child die. It is important for the child to realize that our love for the "really, really me" of the person goes on and that we can't turn love on and off like an electric light. Recently I asked my daughter if she harbored any such feelings when we replaced her dog so quickly. Fortunately, she recalled none.

Many occasions of life can act as lead-ins for a discussion of death with your child. A visit to the cemetery may be helpful. Pictures of relatives who have died, funerals, newspaper items about accidents, and Bible verses can act as springboards. Speak of death as the time when the YOU leaves your body. Talk about where the "really, really me" of the person who has died is now.

Encourage your child to ask questions. Be alert to what the child is actually asking and to the inside feelings *not* being expressed.

Funerals can add mystery to death if your child has no idea of what happens at a service. It is generally best for the child to attend the funeral so as to feel a part of the family experience. After a death stress the support of Christian friends and of one another in the family.

Why Do People Die?

The question, "Why do people die?" may mean, "Are *you* going to die and leave me?" Tell your child that usually people live to be very old before they die. You don't expect to die for a long, long time. Help children realize that they are loved and cared for by many people. Name them, emphasizing their love as well as your own, and that God planned for us to have family and friends who care about us. If children are very disturbed and old enough to understand the subject, you might share any plans you have put in a will, plans that will be carried out should something unexpected happen to you.

Be alert to "missing" times. Feel free to say, "We miss Grandmother, don't we?" Share happy memories. "Grandmother's life is like a beautiful story that we wish would go on forever." Perhaps the child may write a story of a good time shared with Grandmother.

Sometimes children imagine they are guilty of causing someone's death. My father was only three when his mother died, and his father died of pneumonia when Dad was five. It took him many years to work through the guilt that came from feeling that he had caused both deaths. After the death of his mother in childbirth, he heard some women of the country community discussing her illness. They said, "If that big Paul had not insisted that Lizzy hold him all of the time, she might not have died." Then as his father was dying, he was sent to bring a wet cloth to his bedside. When he returned, he was told by those helping his father, "It's too late. He's already dead." The boy's mind reasoned that had he been quicker, he might have saved his father. The death of both parents lay heavy on him as a boy, and he had no one with whom to share the weight.

After the death of someone who has been ill, the child can become terrified of becoming ill and dying. Stress that God is a loving God who intends that our bodies be strong and healthy and repair themselves. It is usually only when we are very old or not very strong, or when the scientists have not discovered the right medicines to make us well that an illness cannot be healed. With the young child it is best not to emphasize a person being tired or sick preceding death.

Always give the simple, physical reason for death. If we speak of God taking the person away to a better life, then children can grow to hate God because God is seen as having taken away someone that the child loved dearly. Or they may fear that God will take a parent away, too. God does not strike us down. The disease or accident was the cause of the death. Sometimes the doctors cannot find the right medicines to help God to make the person well.

Encourage your child to ask for extra love from you, the parent, at the time of a death. The support of your love helps the child, and it helps you, too.

Share your belief that God has a plan for us after death. Sometimes we wonder just what the plan is, but we know it's good because we know of God's goodness. Our bodies will be different, as a seed must die to produce a plant. The term "live forever" helps a child to think of heaven as a life lived in love, here on earth and beyond earth. Paul's suggestions for parallels in nature in 1 Corinthians 15:35-41 may help clarify your thoughts on this.

Tragic deaths which we cannot understand cause questions in adult minds as well as in children's minds. Why does God allow destructive storms? Why are there wars that kill people? Why didn't God stop the drunk man who was driving the car so that it wouldn't hit my friend?

During recent years we have learned more and more about our world. We have learned about diseases that used to kill people, and we have learned how to prevent the diseases and how to heal some people. Many new inventions help us to know about the weather and how to predict changes. There is much that God seems to have left for us to learn about. God gave us minds to use so that we could discover more about our world.

Unfortunately, we often hear the explanation of a tragic death as "God's will," and we are told that we must "bow under the will of God." This concept shapes God as a vengeful God, one who moves us about like playing pieces in a game. But the Bible tells us that we are created in the image of God. We have the ability to decide, to create, and to use that which we create. Sometimes we use it wisely and sometimes not so wisely. But God did not make us puppets.

Leslie Weatherhead in his book *The Will of God* defines God's will in three parts: "The intentional will of God means the way in which God pours himself out in goodness, such as the true father longs to do for his son."[6]

But because God intentionally gave us free will, "because man's free will creates circumstances of evil that cut across God's plans . . . there is a will within the will of God, or what I call 'the circumstantial will of God.' "[7]

Weatherhead stresses that we can follow God's direction through the circumstances as they develop and thereby work toward fulfilling God's original plan—the ultimate will of God is never defeated when we walk with God.[8]

Helping your child face death, or any other life experience, and grow in faith is a gift that often returns itself. Crystal Zinkiewicz tells the story of how her daughter gave her a faith gift.

> That particular Sunday fell just three months after my mother's death; it would have been her fifty-fifth birthday. My Sunday school class had placed flowers on the altar in celebration of her life. I sat through the opening exercises of the Sunday morning worship service in misery. The wound was opened afresh. The tears would not stop.
>
> My seven-year-old daughter sat next to me, drawing on the back of the offering envelopes as she does every Sunday. But this Sunday she sat closer and worked harder. The order of worship provided only momentary distraction from my tears. I mumbled through the prayer of confession and the responsive reading. I could barely sing the hymn.
>
> I felt a tug on my arm. Ellen pressed her masterpiece into my hands. It was a simple cross set in clouds with the words—some misspelled—"He is with her in heaven." I had received a faith gift from my child.
>
> At that moment Ellen did for me what Ed and I have tried to do for her all these years. She had made a connection between a life experience and faith.[9]

8
Hi, God! It's Me!

When asked what religious experience she wanted most for her child, a mother answered, "That she experience God as a personal friend. I want her to feel free to turn to God at any time and at any place for help and for her to learn to listen to God's direction." A personal friend is one who knows all about us—what we are like, all our negative as well as our positive features—and likes us anyway.

Yet we have our part of the friendship to develop. I cannot be a complete friend with someone from whom I hide a wrong. Even if my friend knows of my error, and I know that my friend knows, there is a strain on the friendship as long as I don't open up. Then when there is acceptance, a relationship of true friendship develops.

The same is true with God. Often we say, "Since God knows everything, why admit our wrongs?" But until we can admit everything, we cannot be open to receive God's friendship.

Prayer is communication with God, and it both reflects and affects our relationship with God. Our prayers convey to our children, even the very small ones, an awareness of God's presence and an attitude of peace.

Many scholars on prayer compare the progression from "saying prayers" and a mature prayer relationship with practicing strokes on the edge of the pool and swimming confidently in deep water. Children need to practice along the edge as they learn, but they also need to be carried into the water from time to time. They need to experience a total immersion of the friendship of God in order to feel confident in the deep water.

Adoration

Bishop Lance Webb in his book *The Art of Personal Prayer* places adoration of God as the first process of preparing ourselves for a prayer relationship with God. He states, "Prayer at its best is meeting God in conscious, glad attentiveness; and who can meet the almighty, loving, all-wise Lord of the universe without what the saints have called *adoration!*"[1]

In leading our children through their development of prayer, we must "first not ask, but adore."[2] Bishop Webb tells of a preacher's young son who pushed open the door of his father's study, came in, and sat at his feet while the man studied. When the father asked him what he wanted, the boy said quietly, "I don't want nuffin'. I'se only looking at you and lovin' you!"[3]

Adoration is, simply put, looking and loving. God is all-powerful in the total universe, as a nuclear bomb is all-powerful in the world of war, but we could never "look and love" a bomb because its destructive capabilities would terrify us. We cannot adore that which only terrifies and threatens us. God loves us in power. We can adore God.

Praise and Thanksgiving

It naturally follows that the first and primary prayer experiences we wish for our children are of praise and thanksgiving to God. You can pray with very young children even before they understand the words. Your calm voice carries God's love and peace.

Approach prayer with preschoolers as talking to God. The prayer should be spontaneous, not forced. Prekindergartners' prayers are best kept to one sentence. As children move into their "friendship" relationship with God, the prayers will naturally grow to two or three sentences. In fact, children sometimes carry on a regular conversation with God in private.

Feel free to give thanks any time. Give thanks for Saturday when there is no school, for Sunday when we are together as a family and can go to church, and for Monday when Dad has a job to do.

There is no need for any particular form for prayer or any special body position. Prayers may be said with the eyes open as well as closed. The only reason we close our eyes is to shut out distractions and concentrate on God. However, when you find a tiny spring blossom among the grasses of a field, the worship experience will be more meaningful if you thank God with your eyes open, experiencing the joy of God's creation.

"Talk" a prayer with your children as you dress them for the day. Talk about how you are thankful that the child is growing, about the new day God has given us, and the happy times planned for the day.

Sometimes children better understand a mealtime prayer said after eating than one said before the meal. Young children's hunger distracts from the prayer, and all they can think about is completing the ritual of the prayer in order to begin the meal.

When your child comments about a favorite dish you have prepared, feel free to stop in the middle of the meal and express a simple thanks to God.

One family, occasionally during a meal, asks each person to name something he or she is especially thankful for that day. Then they pray a simple prayer, "Dear God, you've heard us tell about all these things we are thankful for. Amen."

Often-prayed, familiar prayers encourage a lack of thought. Vary your mealtime prayers with your children so that the prayers do not become routine. Sing the prayer occasionally. Or your family may hold hands during a mealtime prayer.

Perhaps an adult can begin the prayer, using a litany form, by saying, "We thank you, God, for all you have given us." Then each person may mention one food that they see on the table. "For the milk we drink." After each item the whole family can say, "We thank you, God." At the close, clasp each other's hands and say together, "Amen." This prayer would lend itself to an open-eyed prayer, giving the children opportunity to look at the table and consider what they want to thank God for.

Silent prayer has little meaning to the very young. Listen to children talk to themselves or imaginary playmates, and you will realize that they usually develop their thoughts verbally. This is natural with their prayers.

Because a child usually thinks verbally, one of the best ways to prepare for prayers at the close of the day is to talk together with the child about the day, the parts of the day that were especially nice. Talk about kindnesses others have shown toward the child and kindnesses the child has shown to others. Talk about how God has helped today. By talking together with you before the prayer, children have time to formulate their thoughts. Then you can pray together a simple prayer of thanksgiving.

Meaningful Prayer

As you pray with your child, consider the wording that you use. Many of the words of our adult prayers have no meaning whatsoever for children. At what age does a child understand the word "bless"? Sometimes I'm not so sure that I understand the real meaning of it myself! "Confess" is another word often used in prayers that is not in children's vocabulary. Make an effort to use familiar words so that prayer becomes as natural as talking.

As I noted earlier, the preschooler has trouble distinguishing between the term "Father," used for God, and the father who is Daddy. It takes several years of practice with the language before children can relate to a dual meaning of a word.

When our son was almost three years old, we had pancakes for breakfast one morning. His father said, "These are delicious!"

The boy turned to him with a questioning look but a determined tone in his voice. "They aren't delicious. They are pancakes!" We could not convince him differently. The syrup-dripping cakes could not be delicious because they were pancakes to him.

As adults we are at home with the concept of the Trinity, and many of us interchange the names God and Jesus in our prayers. This causes no conflict for us, but children cannot begin to grasp abstract concepts before the latter part of their elementary years, and they may be confused when we pray sometimes to God and sometimes to Jesus. If we help them to establish a prayer relationship with God, then they will appreciate even more the truths that Jesus taught us about God, and they can move toward understanding the Jesus–God relationship when they are older.

Petitions and Forgiveness

In the later preschool years of your children you can encourage prayers of request for help. Suggest that they pray, "Help me remember to cross the street carefully . . . to take turns . . . to help Sister."

In the older kindergarten years, the child's experience reaches into the community. Incorporate our helpers into the prayers. "Help the doctor to help Johnny to get better." The child begins to pray for others.

Distinguish between asking Daddy for toys and asking God to help us to take turns. Perhaps this is one way in which God and Santa get all mixed up in a child's mind. When the child prays to

God for toys and then asks Santa for toys, they begin to see them as one and the same. Talk about how God works through people for our physical needs. People supply things like toys. God helps us on the inside so that we are happy and make others happy.

Prayer is a private matter, especially for children. There will be times when your child will want to share a praying experience with others, but do not use his or her prayers as a time to show off. Be cautious of asking children to pray before guests until they want to. If you use it as a time to "say your piece," then it becomes an act for acceptance instead of a form of communication with God.

As children enter school and become familiar with the written word, encourage them to compose a written prayer to be used in family worship or to share at a mealtime. Special Christian celebrations are particularly good times for children to write a litany or prayer as you talk together about what the celebration means.

In the first grade our daughter befriended a retarded girl whom other children teased. She often came home concerned about the girl and the way that her fellow classmates treated her. Helping children become alert to problems of others prepares them for understanding and participating in prayers of intercession later. "Bear one another's burdens . . ." (Galatians 6:2).

As children reach school age, their prayers for help with personal problems may become more pointed. We can encourage them in this. All too many times, on the day of a big test, I have caught myself sending a child out the door to school with the words, "Good luck on your test." Luck is certainly not God. God is not magic. How much better it would have been for me to have said, "I'll be thinking about you while you are taking the test, and I'll pray that your mind is open to God's help with what you have learned."

God does not answer our prayers because we pray in a proper style. Your child may think that God works magic if you pray using a prescribed formula each time. The manner in which we pray and the attitude that we develop toward God sets the stage, making us open to God's goodness and plan for us—a plan that is already there. God's plan and guidance wait for our relationship to develop. That's the beauty of Christianity. It is there without begging if we only prepare ourselves to accept it.

Children may pray for someone to be better and then feel that God has failed if the person is not healed. Help them to understand that although doctors are God's helpers, sometimes they don't discover what's wrong soon enough to help, or maybe no one has found the right medicine.

Prayers of forgiveness become important for elementary age children. As children comprehend the meaning of doing wrong, feeling sorry about it, wanting forgiveness, and the pleasure of forgiveness and of restored relationships, they prepare for experiences of prayers of confession.

Besides the simple prayers which reflect a conversational relationship with God, help the older elementary age child to study some of the prayers of formal worship. Use the hymnal and other aids that include prayers from our heritage. Talk together as a family about the meaning of the words as well as the beauty of the language. Special occasions of the year are celebrated with special prayers. Discuss them together, and use them within your family so that they have more meaning when you use them at church.

Personal Devotions

When your child has developed the skill of grasping the meaning of words while reading silently, encourage personal devotions. There are several books for older elementary children that are written with a daily format. Upper Room Publishers publishes *Pockets*, a devotional periodical for children that has activities as well as reading materials.

Locate books on your child's age level about the Bible times, about various aspects of life today, and about other children. Read some of them yourself so that you can discuss them together and share your thoughts. Purchase a Bible that your child can read. By your own example encourage a devotional time.

Provide a book that your child may use to write private thoughts. There are hardbound (record) books with lined pages, available for a nominal price. They may be found in the book or stationery departments of stores. Diaries usually limit the daily space to the bare essentials without allowing flexible pages for each entry. Call the book a "think book" and suggest that thoughts be written spontaneously, instead of having the child stop to compose them in a proper form.

It is important that our children develop a relationship with God while we are still nearby to support them so that when they become independent of us, they can turn freely to God with their needs.

9
Jesus Was a Man

While each [written words of the Bible, doctrines of the church, personal inner experiential convictions] provides us with one aspect of the authority upon which Christian faith is founded, it is God's historic liberating action in Jesus Christ that is the final authority and the foundation for Christian faith. In the life, death, and resurrection of Jesus Christ, God provides us with the basis for understanding, interpreting, and applying our faith story.

At the heart of our Christian faith is a story. And at the heart of Christian education must be this same story.[1]

From the early years of their lives children learn about the Christian faith most effectively by living with persons who express faith in Jesus and in his teachings. Be certain that your child hears adults (including parents) speak of Jesus frequently. Sing songs and tell stories of Jesus. Appreciate pictures which depict parts of his life.

When our children were of early elementary age, my mother arrived one summer for two weeks' vacation, bearing two large scrapbooks and folders of pictures. At some time during each day of her visit, she and our two children gathered around the dining room table, looking over pictures and telling stories from some part of Jesus' life.

After she left, we kept the scrapbooks accessible for the children, and they often sat with them, remembering the stories their grandmother had shared. The events of Jesus' life became real, with no push for the child to grasp adult theological concepts. They appreciated Jesus as a man.

Since then, during their teen years and as they move into

adulthood, we have enjoyed discussions about the meaning of Jesus' life and his revelation of God. The early appreciation of Jesus as a man who showed us what God was like laid the foundation for our later discussions with our children.

Start Simply

We do not force the mysteries of calculus on a child in the first grade. A child must learn to enjoy and trust simpler concepts first. After he or she develops a love for math, then the child reaches for calculus with a desire to learn. He or she will understand the complex mathematical process after experiencing excitement with basic skills and algebra.

Just as we space out mathematical skills, we save the more involved concepts of our faith for an age of greater understanding. The preschool child can best understand Jesus as a man who lived long ago, a man who showed us what God was like. Jesus showed God to us in the way that he acted and in what he told his friends.

Help your kindergartner realize that whenever we do things that Jesus would do and act toward other people in the way that he did, then we are his friends. A simple statement such as, "Jesus taught us to share with others," helps children to become accustomed to relating Jesus to their actions.

Consider your vocabulary when speaking with children about Jesus. Often we talk about Jesus being "good" and wanting us to be "good." The word "goodness" has many connotations. As an adult we can mentally switch to the appropriate meaning. But often the only definition that a child has for goodness comes from our negative statements:

"Be good and don't wiggle."

"Good boys don't ride the bike on the grass."

"I expect you to be good and keep your clothes clean."

Such goodness consists of obeying rules. Rules are important, but they do not create the real loving concern that you hope to develop in your children. By stressing the rules, you only "condition" your child to an accepted behavior. The action does not come from within.

As you talk with children about Jesus, stress his concern and his loving-kindness more than "goodness." Use stories of when Jesus helped others and how he loved them. His actions made others happy. Tell stories of Jesus simply, stressing the kindness of his deeds. Tell about Jesus asking some of the people to become his special friends, or disciples. Enjoy stories of Jesus helping those who were ill. Your child will appreciate a story of the time when other adults asked the children to leave but Jesus told them to stay because he loved them.

When you visit a lake or seashore, share the story of Jesus and his friends when they were tired and got into a boat to go to another shore. They wanted to be away from the crowd, alone to think.

Children enjoy hearing about Jesus feeding a crowd of people. Tell the story simply, using the sixth and eighth chapters of Mark. Help the children relate to a time when they were hungry. Ask, "Do you suppose that there were some boys and girls there who were hungry?" Jesus' friends found someone with food, and Jesus shared the food with all the people there. How do you think the boys and girls felt after eating the food? The opportunity to tell the story and help your child appreciate Jesus' concern for the people might best come after your child has been hungry and has eaten a satisfying meal.

Children have no concept of large numbers until they have worked with them for some time in math. When our son was five years old, he and a friend were fighting a pretend battle with armies and horses. He asked the boy, "What's the number that is something like a million?"

The boy answered, "You mean a dozen?"

His voice reflected satisfaction in discovering the right word as he said, "Yes, there were a dozen of them coming over the hill!"

Young children's lack of experience with large numbers gives them no basis of appreciation for the multitude of people Jesus fed with the loaves and the fishes. Yet they can relate to a hungry child in the crowd of people, listening to Jesus.

The story of Jesus healing the blind man comes alive to children if you play a game of being blind before you tell the story. Help children experience sightless movement about the room. You can ask, "How do you suppose the blind man felt after Jesus made him see?"

Jesus' Miracles

Young children do not understand the laws of nature well enough to comprehend the impact of a miracle. They accept a miracle as possible because, to the young child, everything is possible. Miracles are a matter of fact to them.

Likewise, young children think that magic is possible. But magic is built on illusions, and we do not want our children to confuse miracles with magic. By basing the children's relationship with Jesus on the miracles he performed, they may see Jesus as a magician.

Refer to the stories that involve Jesus' miracles as stories of how Jesus helped other people. With a love for Jesus the man your child will have a good foundation for accepting the miraculous aspects of the incidents at a later time.

The story of Jesus preparing a cookout for his friends is one of my favorites for young children. I tell the story, leaving out the reference to when it took place (after his resurrection) because the purpose in telling the story is to help young children grasp an appreciation of Jesus in relation to something with which they are familiar and to understand Jesus as a person who enjoyed doing things for his friends.

Jesus had been away from his friends for a long time, and the friends missed him. Peter decided that he would go fishing. He thought that he might not be so sad if he went fishing, because he enjoyed being on the boat in the lake. Besides, he remembered many happy days he had spent with Jesus at that lake.

When he told the other friends of Jesus that he was going fishing, they decided to go too.

They fished all night. Now, these men fished differently than we do. They threw nets over the side of the boat. As the boat moved along, they dragged the nets and caught the fish. Although they fished all night, they hadn't caught a single fish as the sun began to rise. They were coming closer to shore, and they saw someone along the edge of the water waving to them.

The person on shore called out to them, "Throw your nets on the other side of the boat, and you will catch fish." The men in the boat said that they had already tried all sides of the boat, but the person on shore told them to try again.

When they put their nets on the other side and pulled them in, they found them so full of fish that they had to ask another boat to come alongside of them and help them pull the nets into the boat. Those nets were usually heavy when they caught just a few fish. But this time there were so many fish that the nets were breaking!

Slowly they came to shore with their heavy catch of fish. As they came closer they saw the person who had called to them; he was bending over a fire and cooking something. They began to smell fish cooking, and they realized how very hungry they were. They had been fishing all night, and now as they smelled the fish cooking over the fire, their stomachs growled.

Then suddenly Peter said, "That's Jesus!" And he jumped into the water and swam to shore.

Jesus' friends were so happy to see him again! It had been such a long time since he went away. He had known that they would be hungry, and he had cooked a breakfast of fish. (See John 21:1-14.)

Other Concepts

You can help children appreciate the traditions of the Bible by pointing out the differences in the clothing, houses, and customs of Jesus' time and now. Jesus did not attend churches or schools the way we have them today, but the buildings where he learned and worshiped were called synagogues and temples. Share our Hebrew-Christian heritage.

Before they reach school age, children have little understanding of people of past years and different places. When your child begins to study past civilizations in school, you can share the Hebrew customs. Take your lead from the school.

Before they reach the later elementary years, children will have difficulty with a chronological view of Jesus' life. However, in the early elementary years they begin to understand different segments of his life. Jesus was a teacher. He was a friend, and he was also concerned for other people's health. He thought that all of the person was important: the body, the mind, and the part that is the "really, really me." Reemphasize that Jesus was sent to show us the love of God, and we want to be like him.

Sometime during the first three years of school, your child can begin to understand Jesus as ever living and helping us today. He helps us when we remember what he taught us. He helps us because he told us about God.

By the fourth grade, children begin a period of hero worship. If they have had opportunities to learn about Jesus as a man in their earlier years, Jesus easily becomes a hero during these years. Help your children to develop a conscious effort to use Jesus' teachings every day in life. Children of this age can begin to understand the spiritual difference that Jesus' life made in the world.

The Trinity

The concept of the Trinity is something with which many of us struggle even as adults. There is no way to explain it to children who are not ready to grasp abstract thought. Even if you tell them about it and they seem to accept your explanation, they do not understand the religious significance of it. As adults we appreciate God as Creator, Redeemer, and Sanctifier (the last term means one who makes holy). In the young child's thoughts the term "spirit" gets all mixed up with Halloween spirits.

It is better to work toward helping children experience God in the three ways, and then they can label the Trinity later. God is our creator who supplies our needs. God planned life and the world. We remember the God that Jesus showed us. God is loving and makes us feel happy with one another. Today God helps us to become better people in everything that we do. Share the three persons of God separately, and later children will be able to label them as God the Parent, Son, and Spirit.

The older elementary child can begin to work with the abstract concept of the Trinity. Jesus showed us God. Some believe that he was God, others that he was a man who let God work through him. Talk of your own belief, but let your children develop their belief. If they arrive at the belief themselves, it will be strong. Remember that they must work through the early stages of faith (experienced, affiliated, and searching) before accepting an owned faith. No theological position needs to be decided immediately. The important thing is that Jesus showed us God and showed us the way that we should live as Christians.

The concept of atonement may not be understood until adulthood. Older elementary age children can begin to grasp the idea that God through Jesus experienced human life and therefore can help us. We can relate better to God when we realize that as Jesus he struggled with many of the same problems we have. He had people who didn't like him and called him undesirable names. Jesus went through a period of struggle as he decided how he should show God to the people. Should he live a life close to God and help people to see God through him? Or should he throw himself down off the temple in Jerusalem and have angels break his fall, using a flashy performance to show that he was God's Son?

Christmas

Jesus lived in the everyday world. We can relate to him because he was human. He was even born like any other new baby. In our frantic preparations for the most popular of our Christian seasons, we often miss the purpose of the celebration. Even when we stress the birth of Jesus, we fail to talk about why we celebrate his birth.

Children are attracted to babies, and it is easy to dwell on the babyhood of Jesus at Christmastime. One of the best ways to help our children understand the reason for our festivities is to refer to Christmas as the time we *remember when* Jesus was born. Using this term puts the birth in its perspective. It relates the man Jesus, whom the children have learned to love, to the time of his birth. Speak of it as Jesus' birthday. Children realize that birthdays are celebrated by adults.

At children's birthday celebrations we talk about how they have grown and what has happened during the past year. At Jesus' birthday it can be natural to talk about what Jesus' life meant to us and how he made people happy. This need not take away from the excitement of the Nativity story. In fact, you need only to add a postscript to the story, saying, "Jesus grew older and learned to walk and talk, just as you did. His parents loved him as we love you. When he was old enough, he went to school, too. Then he became a big man and told people about God."

Stress the fact that Jesus' birth is important *because* of the man he was when he grew up. During Advent, the preparation for Christmas, we *tell* about Jesus' birth and about Jesus as a man. At Christmas we *celebrate*.

Throughout the Advent season use several translations of the biblical account of Jesus' birth. Hold an open Bible at times when you tell the story in your own words, saying, "This is one of the stories in the Bible." Doing this helps children realize that the story comes from the Bible.

The child needs to hear the common words in order to grasp the story. A young boy had the part of an angel in the drama of the Nativity one year. He had only one line, but he worked hard to learn the line. There was one word that puzzled him. He went to his teacher.

"I learned my line—'I bring you good tidings of great joy,' " he said. "But I don't know what the word 'tidings' means."

The teacher explained that good tidings was the same as good news, and the boy seemed satisfied with the explanation.

When the time came for the pageant, the angel stepped up to the shepherds and raised his hand. There was a long pause.

Suddenly the boy smiled as he remembered what the words meant. He spoke with an excited voice, "Boy, have I got good news for you!"

There are also other Christmas stories and songs, built around the biblical account, but which are not biblical in fact. These are lovely and help to give us a feeling of the ordinary nature of Jesus' birth. However, consider these stories for what they are. Tell your child that these are pretend stories (legends). The authors imagined something that might have been. When your child asks for such a story to be read, speak of it as one of our might-have-been stories.

Other stories and songs for Christmas are just for fun. Many of these have become customs. They are all part of the fun things that we do at Christmas. Enjoy them, but refer to them for what they are—the fun customs that we have added to our Christmas celebration.

The fact that something is not strictly biblical is no reason for us not to enjoy it as a part of our celebration of Christ's birth. My grandfather refused to allow his family to celebrate Christmas at all. They were required to work in the south Georgia fields that day, just like any other day of the year. His reasoning was that we have no actual proof that Jesus was born on December 25. As far as we know, it might have been July 25.

John 1:1-10 refers to Jesus as the light which came into a dark world. Although we have no proof of the exact date of Jesus' birth, it is fitting that Christians in the past decided to celebrate the coming of our spiritual light near the longest night of the year.

With all of the commercial emphasis on Christmas, children can become tense with excitement and hard to live with as they await Christmas Day. By developing traditions within your family, however, spaced throughout the Advent season, you can bridge the waiting period with smaller occasions.

Establish a set day to begin your preparation for Christmas. Some families begin with a special breakfast on the first Sunday of Advent. If the table is set and preparations laid the night before, then the meal runs smoothly.

Remove all fall decor from the house, and add simple Christmas decorations. Pack an early Advent house-trimming box to be used at this time. You might include the makings of an Advent wreath, purple candles and place mats, special pictures, or a centerpiece. Don't be tempted to decorate your house all at once to "get it over with." If articles are brought out at various times during the Advent season, the meaning of Christmas is renewed with each addition.

Shop for the poinsettia on a specified day; decorate with holly and greens at another time. Make the hanging of the door wreath a special occasion. Spend a day making Christmas chains to brighten the house. Plan to make sugar cookies one afternoon after school, but mix up the dough the night before. Throughout the day at school your children will anticipate the baking fun.

Our family has baked gingerbread men each year, making a hole in the top of each cookie and looping a ribbon through it to hang on the tree. We decide together which friend should receive one of our men, and as long as the children were in elementary school, one cookie went to each teacher.

Inexpensive crèche figures that children can enjoy handling make an effective simulated learning experience for your children. You might consider using only the principal characters at first, and then later in the Advent season add the shepherds; hold off the wise men until after Christmas Day. Or you may prefer that all the figures be available throughout the season for the children to use as they relive the complete Christmas story.

In our family the crèche is usually the first sign of Advent. We have even unpacked it as early as Thanksgiving when out-of-town relatives visited us at that time. When the children were young, we selected a special crèche set that could be purchased by the individual piece. Each year we planned which figure we would add to the scene. The anticipation and excitement over the new figure renewed the meaning of the crèche each Advent.

Once the crèche set was completed, we began purchasing or making a special ornament for each child every year. As they leave home and establish their own family Christmas traditions, the ornaments will go with them, bridging their Christian heritage into a new generation.

By having set times and anticipating and preparing for Christ's birthday throughout the season, you remove the emphasis on the gifts of Christmas Day and center your thoughts on the preparations along the way.

If you enjoy certain cultural traditions, continue to follow them. Discuss with your children when and where the tradition began and whether it is a part of the biblical Christmas or a part of our just-for-fun celebrations.

Santa has become a permanent part of the just-for-fun celebrations of Christmas. When children ask if he exists, you might tell them that a man named Saint Nicholas did live long ago and gave gifts to others because he loved Jesus. We remember him at Christmas, how he gave gifts in secret, not letting the receiver of the gift know that he had given it. Thinking about Santa Claus is fun, and we call him the "spirit of giving." Help children think about the joy that Santa has in *giving* gifts. Bring out the point that Santa represents the *giving* of gifts, not the getting. Think together about ways that they can be Santa. Help them to plan little "Santa surprises" for other members of the family throughout the Advent season.

As you plan for purchasing or making gifts, talk about how the other person will be happy with the gift the child selected. Look forward to Christmas, and help your child to imagine how the person will feel when the gift is opened. Express pleasure and approval in the gift selection. Comment on how your child thought about the person in selecting the gift.

At our house we have a set rule that no one leaves the bedroom area on Christmas morning until everyone is dressed and ready for the day. The stockings and any unwrapped gifts are available before breakfast, but everything else waits until we finish our special meal.

Some families plan their breakfast to be a birthday-type celebration, with coffee cake and candles. They sing "Happy Birthday" to Jesus. Other families share a birthday cake at the dinner meal.

The emphasis on giving gifts instead of receiving can be underscored if you take turns opening your gifts. By opening the gifts slowly, with everyone watching as each gift is opened, the giver of the gift can notice how the recipient likes the gift. When Christmas becomes a rush from one gift to another, take a break.

David and Elizabeth Gray in their book *Children of Joy* recommend spreading the gift opening through the day or even holding onto most of the children's gifts from the parents, and spacing them out over the Twelve Days of Christmas. The Grays have even purchased token gifts to be used during the twelve days, thereby taking the Christmas spirit into the new year.

If you make Christmas a season for remembering the birth of the man Jesus, then after Christmas Day you can naturally talk about the life that the Christmas birth began. Plan to carry the thoughts of Christmas through the year. Make Christmas Day the first of twelve days of celebration and singing.

When the new year arrived last year, we hated to take our wreath off the front door. Instead, every two months we have rewrapped our straw wreath in a ribbon typical of the season and added a snowman, a valentine, a sprig of flowers, or some colored leaves. When we see the wreath, it reminds us of Christ, whose life has been and always will be. Like a circle his life has no beginning and no end. The changing of the ribbon and wreath decorations reminds us that we take Christ from Christmas into every season.

Easter

Without Easter we would have no reason to celebrate Christmas. Easter should be the highlight of Christian celebration.

As Advent is the preparation period for Christmas, so Lent is a time of getting ready for Easter. As adults we use the Lenten period to prepare ourselves mentally and spiritually for Easter. Older children and youth can understand some of our study and discussion. All of your family can gain, however, if you center the preparation around young children. Although the young child cannot understand the theological meaning of Passion Week and Easter, you can lay a foundation and include him or her in the church family celebration of joy.

During the pre-Easter weeks our whole world seems, as if on tiptoe, to anticipate new life. Life, hidden for months during the winter, begins to burst forth. Review the suggestions made for springtime in chapter 4, and alert yourself to opportunities to share new life with your child.

Use the week before Easter to read stories about Jesus and talk about "when Jesus grew up and became a man." Young children need this transition time to develop their perspective of the baby Jesus and the man. Stories of Jesus can naturally lead to Palm Sunday, the exciting celebration when friends of Jesus held a parade.

For children under kindergarten age, explain that we are happy because it is springtime and a time that we remember Jesus. As Easter draws nearer, talk about Easter as a day when we are especially happy and think about Jesus.

Many of the traditionally fun things you may do with your children at Easter do not directly relate to the resurrection of Christ. But just as the Christmas season brings just-for-fun celebrations, you can enjoy just-for-fun activities at Easter.

Help your children experience the joy of Easter. Then when they wonder about what it really means, you can move to the death of Jesus. The early elementary age child will understand if you speak briefly of people who didn't like what Jesus taught so they put him to death. But his friends felt he was still near.

Explain that some people thought Jesus was wrong all through his life. He did things that they thought were against their laws. When the child asks who killed Jesus, avoid quick answers such as "The Jews." But rather, in fact, recall that Jesus was a Jew. His enemies were the people who killed him. They were people who didn't think he was teaching about God.

The older elementary child can realize from this that it is possible for the minority to be right. Although the majority of the people of that time believed that Jesus should be crucified for teaching wrong ideas about God and that the early Christians should be persecuted for believing in Jesus, we now know that the minority was right.

The theological answer of Jesus' death for our sins cannot be grasped until much later. The child may "learn" the explanation and be able to respond with the answer, but any real understanding does not occur until the end of their elementary years or during their teens when they think abstractly.

Tell the story of the resurrection. We believe that God wouldn't let Jesus stay dead. He won't let us stay dead either. He'll provide a different type of life, but we won't be dead. Older elementary age children can deal better with the physical or spiritual aspects of the resurrection.

Feel free to rehearse Easter hymns of joy throughout the week before the Easter celebration. Then your children can relate Easter week with Easter Sunday in their minds.

Even in a family with young children you can begin preparation for Easter on Maundy Thursday. "Maundy" comes from the Latin word *mandare*, meaning "command." We are eating a meal as Jesus commanded us. At supper that night, talk about what people ate in Jesus' day. Use unsliced bread, and tear off pieces, as was the custom then. Think about how sad the friends of Jesus were when he told them that this would be the last meal they would eat together.

You might plan to use three old purple candle stubs and one new white candle on your table during the three days before Easter and on Easter Day. Each day light all three of the old candles, saving the new one for Easter. After lighting them on Thursday, extinguish one; on Friday light all three and extinguish two; and on Saturday extinguish all three. In this way you are remembering the days before Easter which were "sad" days. Ask the children each day, "When will we light the new white candle?" Build the anticipation and excitement of joyfully lighting the tall Christ candle on Easter Day.[2]

Good Friday is a day of *remembering* what happened to Jesus. We call it "good" because we know what happened afterwards. We already know the end of the story—that God didn't let Jesus stay dead but raised him. Have simple meals on this day and avoid elaborate snacks. We remember that Jesus died, and so we eat simply.

Tell your preschool and kindergarten age children that the cross on Good Friday tells us of God's love in a special way. The older child will understand that the cross tells us that God's love is greater than any wrong we may do.

When a young child asks why Jesus died, she or he usually wants the factual reason—because people didn't agree with what he was teaching. Explain that at that time, people who were to be killed were sometimes hung on a cross to die.

Leslie D. Weatherhead says the following about God's intention from the beginning that Jesus should die on the cross:

> I think the answer to that question must be No. I don't think Jesus thought that at the beginning of his ministry. He came with the *intention* that men should follow him, not kill him. The discipleship of men, not the death of Christ, was the intentional will of God, or, if you like, God's ideal purpose—and I sometimes wish that in common language we could keep the phrase "the will of God" for the intentional will of God.
>
> But when circumstances wrought by men's evil set up such a dilemma that Christ was compelled either to die or to run away, then *in those circumstances* the Cross was the will of God, but only in those circumstances which were themselves the fruit of evil. In those circumstances any other way was unworthy and impossible, and it was in this sense that our Lord said, "Nevertheless not what I will but what thou wilt."
>
> . . . God cannot be finally defeated, and that is what I mean by his omnipotence—not that everything that happens is his will, but that nothing can happen which *finally* defeats his will. So, in regard to the Cross, God achieved his final goal not simply in spite of the Cross but through it. He achieved a great redemption and realized his ultimate will in as full a sense as he would have done if his intentional will had not been temporarily defeated.[3]

The resurrection shows that whatever we do, God can undo.

Use the Saturday before Easter as a time to "shine" the house for Easter as you would for any joyous celebration. Easter is our Christian festival; treat it as such with decorations and music. Plan special clothes to wear. Stress the reason for wearing special clothes: not to show off but because we are celebrating Easter.

Begin Easter morning by enjoying a festival breakfast with the whole family. Preparations the night before will make the morning run smoothly. Use any of the Easter hymns you might have practiced during the week, and sing the doxology as a prayer. Celebrate with joy!

10
The Bible Tells Us About God and Jesus and His Friends

There is no doubt that the Bible was written for adults. The book contains symbolism that even adults have difficulty handling, and so we cannot expect children to grasp every part of the book. However, it is important that children have experiences with the Bible throughout their lives.

A child may know intellectually all that there is to know about God without really knowing God spiritually. The same is true with the Bible. Children may memorize many Bible verses and learn the answers to questions concerning the Bible, but unless they learn to apply the content of the Bible to everyday life, it serves no purpose. Bible verses are only vehicles to explore the great teachings of our religion. We are concerned that our children apply the Bible to the development of their spiritual relationship with God. We do not want just lip service to the words.

Therefore, we must use the Bible in various ways with different aged children. The preschooler and kindergartner understands best when we paraphrase some of the verses, using language within their understanding. Be certain that the child sees you use and appreciate the Bible.

At times, hold the Bible as you tell children a story in words that they can understand. Share with your preschoolers stories such as the children visiting Jesus, Jesus teaching of God, Jesus enjoying nature, Jesus' breakfast with friends, when Jesus was a baby, and Mary and Joseph caring for Jesus when he was young.

Encourage children to retell Bible stories. Maryann Dotts's book

When Jesus Was Born offers an excellent example of retelling the Advent story. It emphasizes words, sounds, actions, and feelings in such a manner that the child can relate to them. The success of storytelling with children depends upon the use of terms and experiences with which they are familiar. Word repetition is used in Mrs. Dotts's "talk-together" book. For instance, if you have the child say the words, "Walk, walk, walk," with you when you are reading from the page that tells that Mary and Joseph walked to the barn, the child can remember that part of the story each time he or she sees the picture on the facing page. Each page allows the child to participate in this manner.

The Bible can become alive to children of all ages if you use simple drama with the stories. Help them to experience how the disciples threw out their nets and pulled hard to get the big catch of fish. If you ever have an opportunity to seine for fish, take advantage of the chance to feel the pull of the nets against the water.

You need not open the Bible each time you talk with your child about the book. In fact, some of the most remembered biblical concepts shine through in everyday life. You might tell your child, "Thank you for telling the truth about what really happened. The Bible tells us to do that." It is not necessary to quote an exact reference but simply relate the Bible to everyday life.

After I spoke to a group in a church in Kennesaw, Georgia, the minister's wife, whose name was Liz, told me, "My grandfather taught me more about the Bible than anyone else. And he taught it every day, seldom reciting a Bible verse in the exact words."

Her grandfather was a produce farmer, and Liz often went with him to the farmer's market. She sat beside him as he sold tomatoes and beans and turnip greens. As he weighed up a sale, he would turn to his granddaughter and say, "Now, Liz, you put the greens on the scale until it hits the pound mark. And then you reach over and take a little bit more, and you put that on. The Bible tells us to give a full measure."

We do not want our children simply to memorize words from the Bible but, rather, to absorb the truths of the book into their lives.

As your children begin to read, help them realize that we have various translations of the Bible. It was originally written in Hebrew and Greek. Some people understand one way of telling a story better than another way. Sometimes we want to use a translation that tells the story in language that we use every day. Other times we want a translation that we are sure was directly translated from the original. When your children's reading skills improve, expose them to various translations. There are now copies of the New Testament published with parallel translations on one page, so that you can read several versions side by side.

Selecting Biblical Material

In selecting Bible materials to use with your child, consider the religious content, the moral teaching, and the emotional effect on the child. Some of the Old Testament stories may be *about* children but not necessarily stories that will benefit a child. In most of the Old Testament stories the concept of God had not grown beyond one involving fear and vengeance.

Consider the story of the sacrifice of Isaac. Although it is *about* a child, it is not a story *for* children. They might interpret it in two ways. They may be frightened to think that a father would sacrifice a child, or they may believe from the beginning that such a situation would be impossible because of their experience with their own father. Both interpretations miss the point of the story—that Abraham followed God's requests, no matter what they were. Since the story does not improve the young child's appreciation of the Bible, it is best to leave it until the age when the child can understand the theological point.

The story of the baby Moses may likewise be emotionally disturbing to the young child if you tell about the slaughter of the babies. Children relate very closely to babies, and any reference to violence toward a baby affects them personally. However, the story can be used, avoiding mention of the slaughter and emphasizing the sister who cared for the baby.

Another incident of the slaughter of children occurred after Jesus' birth. Until your child can understand the impact of how the Messiah's existence threatened Herod, it is best not to mention it or simply to tell the child that Mary and Joseph took the baby and went to another country because God told them to do this.

Samuel is another Old Testament character that many people believe children enjoy because he was a child at the temple. However, when you use the whole story, a young child may fear being left by parents, as Samuel was left at the temple. I can recall wondering whether my mother might ever leave me with someone else and if I could be happy away from my family. But I was afraid to voice the question.

A better way to share the story would be to begin with Samuel, a boy who lived at the temple with Eli. Say that Samuel loved the temple and enjoyed helping Eli. The boy learned much about God from Eli and enjoyed talking to God.

In any story that you use be certain to stress the affirmative actions of adults toward the children. Younger children (preschoolers and kindergartners) can enjoy the affirmative stories of the Bible just for the sake of a good story. You establish an excitement about the Bible even before the child can understand the content.

Despite all I have said, in a family, children of different ages will hear a Bible story together, but they will respond to it differently. Perhaps the story of Noah and the ark is heard. The preschoolers and kindergartners will receive it as a nice story which we enjoy from the Bible. The elementary age child can grasp the reason behind the building of the ark and the fact that most of the world was bad or ungodly and had to be destroyed and that only the family of Noah and two of every animal were saved.

The rainbow after the flood was a sign of God's promise that no other flood would ever again completely cover the earth. The elementary age children can recall other covenants of God: the covenant with Abraham in which God promised he would be the father of a great people; the one with Moses who was to be the giver of the Law; the one God made with Israel, that God would continue with the people even when they failed to keep faith; our new covenant in Jesus Christ; and our personal covenants which we enter into today, such as joining the church, marrying, and baptizing our children.

Relating to the Bible

The children of today's society sometimes have trouble understanding the examples set forth in the Bible. They might understand better if the stories were told about people moving about in automobiles and working in office buildings. But the primary method of transportation in the Bible times was walking, and one of the common occupations was caring for sheep. Does today's child know a shepherd, such as the one referred to in the Twenty-third Psalm? The extent of most children's experience with a shepherd has been seeing the crèche figure at Christmas.

Do we really understand today what a shepherd does? Do we realize that the sheep would die of starvation if the keeper did not move them about to new land? We speak of the shepherd leading us by still water, but we don't fully comprehend the sentence unless we realize that the sheep will not drink from running water, no matter how thirsty they are. Sheep will die before they will venture into running water to drink, and so the shepherd either has to find a pool of still water or build a dam across the stream so that the water will form a pool for the sheep. It is only after children begin to think abstractly that they can draw comfort from the psalm that means so much to many of us.

The parables are stories that Jesus told. He used examples familiar to his times. It is good for preschool children to become familiar with some of the parables as stories, but, again, the meaning behind the story cannot be grasped until the time of abstract comprehension. Children will enjoy the story of the parables without the meaning. Leave the meaning for later.

Have fun with the story of the sower, dramatizing the way that people sowed seeds long ago. Sometimes we sow grass seed in the same manner. Allow children to help. Later, when they can understand the concepts portrayed, you can build upon the familiar parable.

In talking with your children about the parable of the mustard seed, help the small child to marvel over the tiny seeds and talk about God's plan for growth. The middle elementary age child can begin to grasp the meaning of the parable.

How did you feel about the prodigal son the first time you heard the story? I recall that for years I sided with the older brother, feeling that he was slighted and that the father had not been just. I was unable to put myself into the younger brother's position and thereby missed the reason that Jesus told the story—God's acceptance of us, no matter how we have acted in the past. Stress the excitement over the return and the happiness of the father. As children mature, they can understand that the story depicts an acceptance, as God accepts us.

The age of the character is immaterial; the important thing is the way that the child can relate to the experience. Zacchaeus is one of the favorite stories of children. He was not a child, but the child can identify with someone who was small in stature. Children know what it is like to stand, hemmed in by big people, and not able to see the main attraction. Children know how it feels when others don't like you, and yet someone says, "I will be your friend, anyway."

Appreciate the story itself; as the child matures, the concepts will unfold. The meanings that a child cannot grasp at a young age are better left unexplained until a later date.

The preschooler can learn from you, the parent, that the Bible is an important book. It is a book that tells us about Jesus and about God. Use simple verses at spontaneous times. See the chart on page 120 for suggestions for verses to share with young children. Some of them may need to be paraphrased so that they are better understood.

Before a child can read or handle the mechanics of locating Bible verses, prepare a special Bible with simple verses underlined or highlighted. Place bookmarks in the Bible where these verses are located. On the ends of the bookmarks you may draw simple pictures which relate to the verses. Then children can turn in the Bible to the location and remember the verse even before they can read it. You might draw a picture of clouds or a sunset for Psalm 19:1 or food for Job 36:31*b*. Picture the seashore or shells for Psalm 95:5, and a cornstalk would remind the child of Psalm 104:14*b*. After telling your child about the fish breakfast that Jesus shared with his disciples, draw a picture of fish cooking over an open fire, and place the marker in the Bible at John 21:12.

As your child approaches school age, you may begin to use larger verses, but be sure to use translations that the child understands.

Begin to associate everyday stories that you read or tell with what we learn from the Bible. "The boy in the story was sharing, like the Bible tells us to share."

Use Old Testament stories that exemplify *positive* behavior. Miriam cared for her baby brother, Moses. Samuel received a new coat and said thank you. Ruth gathered grain to share with Naomi. The family prepared a rooftop room to welcome Elisha.

Bible Background and History

At about age six the concept of time has developed. Children understand our references to "next Sunday." They recall previous years and know that Christmas is next winter. However, they are still not able to comprehend the scope of biblical history.

The early elementary child can realize that the Bible has two parts. The Old Testament is the part that Joseph read to the family and that Jesus enjoyed when he was a child. The New Testament tells about Jesus and his friends. The book of Psalms is the hymnbook of the Bible. People sang the Psalms during Jesus' time, and we sing some of them today. "Praise to the Lord, the Almighty" is taken from Psalms 103 and 150. "O God, Our Help in Ages Past" was written by Isaac Watts, using Psalm 90.

The elementary age child can learn about the background from which the Bible comes. Relate situations in the Bible stories to today. We have no roofs on which to sit and watch the stars, but we can sit on the deck or in our backyard on a clear night and see the same stars that the people in the Bible story enjoyed. When we sleep in tents on camping trips or in our backyards, we remember that some of the people in the Bible lived in tents all the time. They had to use tents because they moved about a lot and didn't have trailers as we do today. Jesus helped the lonely; we help the new child at school who must be lonely.

As the child begins to read, be aware of the reading level and select appropriate verses. Make any Bible reading a pleasant experience, not a chore.

Older elementary children can begin to understand that the Old Testament tells the story of the growth of the Jewish understanding of God. Help the child to make the prophets of the Hebrews our prophets. They are a part of our heritage and, as much as the Pilgrims or our ethnic foreparents, helped to form our world today.

The New Testament adds to the developing concept of God. Jesus tells us more about God's loving nature. The latter part of the New Testament is the story of the early church when Jesus' friends told others about him. We can appreciate Jesus through the early disciples' eyes, as we appreciate our early national leaders through the eyes of the historians.

Help fourth or fifth grade children to begin to look on the Bible as a textbook for our lives. God helps us through the Bible. For example, Amos, Isaiah, and Jeremiah hesitated to accept God's call to speak to their people, but they finally followed God's plan. Children can learn obedience from these men. We live by the principles set in the Bible. Help children evaluate their own behavior by Jesus' life.

Now you can begin using Old Testament stories showing wrong behavior, such as Sodom and Gomorrah; Amos and the elite classes which ignored the poor; King David and Bathsheba; Adam and Eve; the jealousy of Cain and Jacob and Esau; the false pride in the story of the tower of Babel; Joseph's brothers selling him into slavery; Moses' action that caused him not to be able to cross into the Promised Land; and the ungodliness of the people in Noah's time.

The older elementary age children have worked with research books in school and understand what a table of contents is. They can group the books of the Bible according to whether they give the law or are books of the prophets, etc.

You can enjoy maps with your older elementary children. They are ready for the historical approach to the Bible. Television documentaries on archeaological findings dealing with biblical times will help older elementary children relate to the Bible. Augment the television specials with conversation about the findings, and feel free to follow up with research as a family.

Use and enjoy the Bible with your children. Use it as it was intended to be used, as a guide and a resource book, an inspiration for life. Be careful not to imply that the Bible is a good luck charm. Placing the Bible in a pocket does not keep enemy fire away during a war, and dropping a Bible will not bring bad luck.

The Bible is our greatest tangible heritage, and we want our children to learn to use it as an aid in their growth toward God.

11
The Church and Your Child

Today we begin early to prepare our children for the areas of life which we consider important. Children move from tumbling classes to dance workshops, and some Little League sports begin in first grade. We prepare children for mature physical activity. However, do we place the same emphasis on the preparation for Christianity?

You, as a parent, can lay the foundation for your child's future relationship with the church. Speak affirmatively of experiences and feelings about the church. When a child has parents that are happily active in the church, the child is likely to be happy in the church also.

The Church Is Important

The church is the only institution in today's society that includes people from all ages. Help your child appreciate all members of the church. Seek out and develop family friendships within the church, and plan experiences outside the church with these friends.

Point out to your child that we enjoy our church and that there are churches everywhere we go. When you are driving on a trip, count the churches along the road. There are Christians all around the world who follow Christ's teachings.

Take advantage of the church's role in assisting your children's religious growth. Visit the sanctuary as a family at a time when there is no service. With the young children who spend Sunday mornings in the nursery, talk about what you do during a church service. Arrange for them to attend part of a service with you occasionally.

Even young children can appreciate knowing that the Bible on the pulpit which the minister uses is the same as the one at home. For older children who can read, take along a Bible from home of the same translation as the pulpit Bible and let the children see that they are the same.

Enjoy the pictures or stained-glass windows that your sanctuary may have. Young children cannot understand symbols, but they will appreciate the scenes in the windows. Familiarize yourself with the stories that the windows depict, and tell one of the stories. If you have several stained-glass picture windows, plan for additional visits to share the other stories. Explain to your children that the stained-glass windows were first made when most people could not read. The priests would tell the people the stories, and when they saw the pictures in the windows they could remember the stories instead of reading them from the Bible, as we do today.

If your church uses a Chrismon tree during Advent, plan a time when you can take the children into the church and view the tree up close. Tell young children that the special ornaments on the tree remind us of Jesus' birth in different ways, and admire the beauty of the tree with them. Older children can begin to appreciate some of the meanings behind the symbols. Most churches that use Chrismon trees have the explanations available.

Symbols and Rituals

The church uses symbols in its architecture as well as in artwork and design. As a family spend some time studying the symbols you find in the sanctuary. Your church library or your church school resource literature will have helpful books on symbols. *The Young Readers Book of Christian Symbolism*, by Michael Daves, is one of the best sources available.

Discuss the rituals and creeds of your church. Enjoy hymns at home that your congregation often sings during the service. When children are familiar with the hymns and various parts of the service and have opportunity to ask about their meanings, children become a part of the worshiping family of Christ.

The colors which we use during various seasons of the church year are symbols. Some families purchase place mats of each seasonal color for their home use, thereby reminding themselves of the church each day at home. During the meals talk about the reasons you are using that particular place mat. On your wall calendar mark the days that the colors will change.

The Sunday Service

If your church mails the Sunday bulletin during the preceding week, review the upcoming service and read the Scripture together. After the service take a bulletin home and reread the Scripture, talking about some of the points which the minister brought out. If taking notes during the sermon will help you discuss the service at home, don't hesitate to do so. Older elementary children will grasp the sermon better if they make notes.

Help your child relate to the pastor as one of God's helpers by inviting him or her into your home. Perhaps you will want to invite the minister's family for a meal and enjoy an evening together with them. When your children know the minister's family, they can understand why we give money to the church to pay the minister. If the minister spent all of his or her time working on a job somewhere in order to care for his or her family, there would be no time to do what we need the minister to do in the church.

Some churches plan a special time during the service when the children come to the front of the sanctuary and gather around the minister for a few minutes of conversation. Because children under sixth grade seldom think abstractly, many of the "object lessons" often used during this experience float right over the heads of the children and are more effective for us adults. But a positive result of such an experience is the close relationship which develops between the child and the minister.

Iris V. Cully, the first woman appointed to the faculty of Yale Divinity School and a pathbreaker in religious education, states:

> The one thing preachers should not do (but frequently do) is to give object lessons. Young children think concretely and do not make abstract deductions from a concrete example. [Jean] Piaget's studies . . . indicate that children think concretely until the age of almost twelve. But the whole point of the object lesson is to make an abstraction from the concrete. The teller shows children something that will hold their attention, then tells them that God (or the Bible or the Christian life) is like that object. At best they will be confused. Usually they will forget the explanation almost immediately and remember only the object. What a waste of time—unless entertainment was the whole point![1]

The ministers who use simple Bible stories or stories from children's personal experiences speak more directly to children. While holding a Bible, the minister may tell one of the stories in simple words. Or the minister may talk about enjoyable times that children have in church or with their families and share God's plan for families or God's plan for different parts of the world. Occasionally the children might be asked to share one thing for which they are thankful and close with a simple prayer of thanksgiving.

By talking about experiences that children know and understand and drawing those experiences into God's plan, the minister has helped the child to build a bridge between Sunday and the rest of the week.

The Church School

Take advantage of your children's church school classes. Be aware of what's happening in the classroom. Talk with the teacher, and learn about curriculum plans so that you can supplement the learning at home. Use some of the prayers and songs that the class enjoys at church. Let children know that you think their class sessions are important.

If your children are absent, find out what was missed and assist in making it up. If your children follow your church's course of study through each year, by the time they reach adulthood, the complete Bible will have been covered, sometimes several times. However, when you miss several Sundays, spaces appear in the children's curriculum. It is important that you as the child's primary teacher arrange to supplement the time that was missed.

Most classes have some sort of take-home papers that relate to the current session. Set aside a specific time during the week to read the stories to your children, or familiarize yourself with the older child's paper and discuss some of the articles or stories.

The preschool child learns to love the church through happy experiences. When your children are moving into new classes or you plan to attend a new church for the first time, make arrangements to visit the classroom with them at some time when the class is not in session. Walk around the room together and talk about the different toys available. Sit down on the small chairs and read a story from one of the books. The preschool child begins to associate God and Jesus with the church. The church is where we learn more about God and Jesus. We sing songs and hear stories about them.

Caring About the Church

Kindergartners begin to feel a responsibility for their church. They learn to treat the church building as a special place because it is enjoyed by the church family. Encourage them to pick up trash they may see and to help arrange the chairs and put toys away before leaving the classroom. Visit the furnace room and the electric meter.

Acquaint your child with the workers of the church. When children know the janitor who cleans the floor, they are more understanding about caring for the upkeep of the building. If you can, arrange for the child to help some with the care of the church from time to time, either by helping someone in charge or by working with you as a family.

Some families take on the responsibility, as a family project, of weeding and planting certain flower beds at the church. One family I know decides on a specific task each year. When the nursery needed new curtains and paint, they sewed and painted together as a family, providing the materials out of their tithe.

As children approach school age, they can understand that we share our money gifts for many things that we need in the church.

Arrange for opportunities for your children to learn about the ongoing program of the church. You might visit the church office and see the records that are kept. Look at the list of the number of people who come to church on each Sunday and the records of the people who are members of the church. Locate your family's name on the official record.

Perhaps your church has a map that shows where the different church families live in the community. Locate your own address on the map so that the children realize that your family is represented.

View the order forms for literature. Talk about how we help to pay for our literature by placing money in the offering plate.

Talk about how the minister uses a car, the books he or she needs, and the fact that he or she has a family. If the minister is to give his or her days to the church, we must pay to help provide for his or her family. We give money to our church to help in all these ways.

The elementary child can begin to experience ways that our church reaches into the community. Arrange to visit shut-in members of the church, and encourage your children's classes to visit a nursing home as a group.

The offering time is a form of worship. It is a time when we give God back some of the money that we have. The older elementary child can understand that it is because of the abilities that God gave us that we are able to earn money for our family, and we want to give some of it back to the church to show that we thank God.

Once children begin earning a little money, encourage them to put some aside from each payment to be used in some way for the church or for other Christian charities that need financing.

As the older children grasp the meaning of history, they can begin to appreciate our church heritage as a part of God's plan throughout the centuries. When certain eras of history are studied in school, remember the historical events of the church that parallel that time. Martin Luther reacted to the church authority during the time that European countries were expanding into the New World. Joan of Arc died for her faith during Henry VI's rule over England. John Wycliffe's translation of the Bible was finished in England during the time of the Ming Dynasty in China.

Celebrate various seasons of the church year at home. The young child will appreciate times when we celebrate as Christians. As children develop, they can move into a full appreciation of our celebrations.

Pentecost is one occasion we often overlook. It is actually the birthday of our church. You might plan a birthday celebration at home on Pentecost Sunday. The older children can begin to grasp the significance of this important event.

An ecumenical awareness is important for today's Christians. You can develop an ecumenical foundation by visiting other church buildings. While you are away from your own home, take part in another service. Stress that we have different churches because people have different beliefs, but we all believe in the same God. By learning about other people's beliefs, we become more familiar with our own. Introduce the term "ecumenical" during the child's latter elementary years.

As your child begins to study about people from other countries, offer stories and information about the Christian church around the world. You may be able to set up a letter exchange with a missionary or a family from another country. Such a contact will help children realize that, although we speak different languages and have different customs, God made us all and we are all a part of the larger Christian family.

Baptism or Dedication

In many churches baptism is one of the first sacraments a child experiences. Most churches that do not practice infant baptism plan some kind of dedication for the young child.

Talk to your children about how happy you were when they were born and that you wanted to thank God for them. Share the story of Jesus' dedication at the temple. Mary and Joseph were thankful for their baby. Explain that during a baptism or dedication service the parents tell the friends at church that they will do everything they can to help their child to know God better. In the congregational response all the friends in the church say that they will also help the child. Tell your children that when they were baptized or dedicated, they became a special part of the church.

Be sure to include an older child in the baptismal or dedication service of the younger brother or sister. By sitting in the pew with the rest of the family and special friends or by standing beside you during the service, older children can appreciate their part in the church family. It also gives them opportunity to experience a service much like the one held at their dedication, which they cannot remember.

Believer's baptism for youth will be dealt with later in this chapter when we consider confirmation.

Communion

Churches offer Communion to children at various ages. Your church may request that children wait for Communion until they become full members. Others have special preparation classes for children before they receive their first Communion. Some churches leave the decision of when a child participates in Communion with the parents. In any case, be sure that your children have some explanation of the sacrament as soon as they are aware of the service.

Infancy may seem early to consider a child's preparation for Communion. Happy mealtimes, however, offer a beginning. For the infant the satisfaction of his or her hunger gives the baby one of the primary pleasures in life. It is important that this enjoyment continue as the child develops.

Praying together as a family prepares children for Communion. Our conversations with God at the dinner table set the mood for later Communion experiences. These prayers must relate to the child's life. Give them conversational nature.

The best teaching tool for any child is parental example. Early childhood learning takes place as you set a pattern of happy Communion experiences in your family. You need not wait for the child to become "of age" to approach the subject. The time to begin is now.

Five-year-old Mendy helped her sister and brother set the table. The excitement of the day shone in her eyes as she carefully placed the napkins beside the plates. The pastor and his family were coming for dinner, and everyone helped with the preparation in some way.

During the meal Pastor Athboy told Mendy how much he enjoyed eating with other Christians. Meals with other families often happen at special occasions. Sometimes it's a birthday, Thanksgiving, Christmas or Easter. A cake makes any birthday meal complete. Thanksgiving and Christmas dinners usually include turkey and some families enjoy a ham at Easter.

To Mendy's surprise the pastor talked about communion being a special meal. Jesus had a last meal with his disciples in the Upper Room. They had bread and a wine much like our grape juice. That's why we celebrate communion with other Christians. It's another way to remember Jesus.

After the meal Pastor Athboy picked up one of the rolls from the bread basket. That morning Mendy had helped her mother knead the dough for the rolls. Now the pastor broke the roll and passed it around the table, saying, "Just like Jesus did in the Upper Room I ask you to take some of this bread and eat it in memory of him."

As Mendy's brother passed the roll, she felt a warm happiness inside. She took a small piece of bread and passed the roll to Mother. She knew that Jesus loved her although he was not there to tell her so.

After everyone had eaten a piece of the roll, the pastor took a glass of milk. "Milk and bread and other food make our bodies strong. Jesus said that God can do more for us than even food and drink. Drink some of the milk, and we will remember Jesus together."

Such experiences offer a personal feeling toward communion. The child relates the warm, happy family experience to the communion service as she grows in her knowledge of its meaning.[2]

Preschool and kindergarten children cannot understand the theological concept of the Communion service, but they can appreciate the fact that it is our way of remembering Jesus, by having a meal together. Talk about how happy Jesus and his friends must have been when they ate together.

As the children mature, they can understand that we have Communion because we remember the last meal that Jesus had. He asked us to drink the wine and eat the bread, remembering that he had to die so that we could know more about God. The words the minister says before we take Communion remind us to think about our lives and remember whether we are following Jesus and acting in the ways he taught us.

Feel free to discuss Communion as a family or privately with each child. After a Communion service or as you prepare any meal with your child, you might ask: "Why do you think we enjoy

Communion as a happy experience? How often do we have Communion? Why do we have it then? Why is Communion important? Do you think it helps those who take Communion?"

Discuss the Scriptures which come to mind with Communion. The Old Testament story of the Passover found in Exodus 12:1-20 acts as the Jewish foundation for our sacrament. In the New Testament the following Scriptures may be used: Matthew 26:26-29; Mark 14:22-25; Luke 22:14-20; and 1 Corinthians 11:23-26.

Think with children about the different people around the world today who participate in our Christian sacrament of Communion. Help them realize that we are all Christians, members of a large family.

Try this experiment in order to point out the sharing experience of a meal together and the fact that a meal includes more than just eating. For one meal, or a part of a meal, send everyone with his or her own dinner into different rooms of the house. Then when you come back together, perhaps for dessert, talk about the difference in eating the same food alone and with others. A meal includes not only food but also a sharing together.

Consider projects or activities you can develop to increase your child's involvement in Communion. You might make banners, murals, and mobiles. Prepare a family devotion for use at breakfast before Communion service at church.

One of our family's most meaningful experiences took place the fall after our children first began to participate in Communion. Our church had just recently begun using the common loaf of bread for the service. We asked the minister if we might provide the bread for our Thanksgiving Communion service. The day before the service we used our favorite french bread recipe and made the loaves. The children experienced an even deeper meaning toward Communion as they partook of the very loaves they had pounded and kneaded on our kitchen counter.

When discussing the Passover, children enjoy preparing some Passover food. Perhaps a Jewish friend of the family will share a recipe with you. Or you might use this one for Passover Banana Cake.

Passover Banana Cake

7 eggs
1¼ cups sugar
1 ripe banana, mashed
⅔ cup potato starch
Dash of lemon juice (optional)

Beat six egg whites until stiff. Beat yolks plus one whole egg. Add mashed banana and sugar to yolks and beat with mixer. Beat in potato starch and lemon juice. Fold in egg whites. Bake in angel food pan in a slow over (325°) for one hour.[3]

Each time you relate their everyday life to Communion, you bring the experience closer to children. Create and search out opportunities to share the meaning of this important sacrament of our faith with your child.

Confirmation or Believer's Baptism

At about age eleven or twelve children begin to understand commitment and are "stretching" in their comprehension of salvation. You, as parents, need to be tuned in to the clues of spiritual growth. Be alert to questions your children ask about the church, and encourage them to seek out help as they move into a life of commitment to Christ.

If your children received infant baptism, this will be a time of confirming the vows taken for them at their baptism. If the rite of baptism is held in your denomination when your children can make their own decision, then you will need to help them understand the declaration of faith that believer's baptism affirms.

Be aware of your children's training for this important step and let them know that you are interested. Work with the children at home, using the materials provided.

I joined the church many years ago, at age five or six. I did not truly understand commitment at that time, but I knew that I wanted to be a part of the church family. I was seeking inclusion, working through my affiliated stage of faith development. My parents wisely allowed me to join and nurtured my development so that later, after a period of searching faith, I came to the commitment end of membership and embraced an owned faith.

Today we try to deal with children's relationship to the church at an early age by stressing the part that they play in the church family NOW, at whatever level they may be, even before full membership. We help children to understand that church membership is one of the steps of our Christian life, a very important step, but that there are other important parts that children can participate in as they prepare for membership.

At home and at church, every activity, every conversation, and every association that children experience sets down another building block of their relationship with God. Watch for opportunities, and share God with your child, pointing out God's plan in every part of the world.

Then you will be able to pray:

> Lord, I'm so glad she doesn't need some formal kind
>   of prayer,
> For Tammy's learned to talk with you
>   while standing on her head,
> And Tammy's learned to feel you near
>   while doing cartwheels in the air.[4]

The Child/The Concept

	NURSERY	KINDERGARTEN
GOD	Associate God with beautiful things. Enjoy creating with God. Associate God with love and care which parents and other adults give. Use the term "God." (The only father the child knows is Daddy.) Encourage the growing desire to talk to God in brief, direct, and simple prayers, as if God were here beside us.	Stress that God loves us and gives us good things. Because God loves us, God wants to be loved by us in return and wants us to share. Teach concept of how God cares for us through others (doctors, farmers, etc.) Stress that we can show our love for God by the things we do. Build on nursery-age concepts.
JESUS	Talk about Jesus, the man who loved children. Say that Jesus told people what God is like. Christmas: Remember when Jesus was a baby; begin with the man Jesus and remember. Easter: Stress new life and loving and appreciating Jesus. Use separate identities of Jesus and God.	Tell stories of Jesus who helped and loved others. Stress that we learn from Jesus. Say that whenever we do things Jesus would do and act as he did, we are his friends. Emphasize that Easter is a time for remembering Jesus. Encourage growth in love for Jesus. Retain separate identities of Jesus and God.

GRADES 1-3	GRADES 4-6
Point out God's plan of cycles. God is dependable. Day follows night; spring always comes.	Explain that we help God's balance in nature.
Stress that God planned night for rest and day for work.	Assure children that God's laws will not change.
Give examples of God's plan for growing.	God's justice is part of God's love.
Explain that because God is good and we are God's children, God expects us to be good. We are good because we love God, not because we are afraid of punishment.	Stress that God depends on responsible people.
	Introduce the child to God as the parent of all peoples; God is all-wise and all-good.
Explain that God forgives us; we forgive others.	Explain that if we fail, God is sorry but still loves us.
Help the child to learn to right wrongs.	Build confidence in God's forgiveness when we are truly sorry.
Stress that God helps us get through problems.	Say that God helps through the wisdom of older persons and the lives of many people.
Say that we help carry out God's purposes by working with God's laws; if we don't get enough sleep, we will get sick; if we are kind to people, they are happy and life is happy for us.	Stress that God helps through the Bible.
	Explain that we learn more about God's world each day.

Say that Jesus was sent to show us the love of God. Encourage a desire to be like Jesus. Encourage the beginning of an understanding of Jesus as ever living and helping today.

Talk about the segments of the life of Jesus: teacher, friend, concerned with others' health.

Talk about customs of Bible times. Begin discussing the Hebrew heritage.

Easter: Near the upper end of this age group, tell briefly that some people didn't like Jesus' teachings and they put him to death, but his friends felt he was still near. Tell the *story* of the resurrection; however, the next age group deals better with physical or spiritual aspects of resurrection.

Retain separate identities of Jesus and God but move toward the Grades 4-6 concept.

Make a conscious effort to use Jesus' teachings every day.

Tell about Jesus' life chronologically.

Talk about the spiritual difference Jesus' life made—he made a better world.

Show Jesus as a hero.

Point out that Jesus showed us God. Some believe he was God, some that he was a man who let God work through him. Talk of your own belief, but let the child develop his or her belief. Help child to realize that this is not something that must be decided immediately. The important thing is that Jesus showed us God and God's ways for us to live. (Older children can grasp the idea that through Jesus God experienced human life and therefore can better help us.)

	NURSERY	KINDERGARTEN
PRAYER	Associate prayer with good things. Pray prayers of thanksgiving and praise. Pray with the child as if you are talking to God. Begin the relationship with God. Use simple language: "you" and "your," not "thee," "thou," and "thine." No particular body position is necessary. Child need not always close eyes. Giving thanks for food after eating it makes more sense to this age child.	Provide some opportunities for prayer. Pray spontaneous prayers. "Talk" to God. Prayer can be two to five short sentences of everyday speech. Pray what the child understands. Religion is private; prayer is not a time to show off. Be cautious of asking child to pray before guests. Evening prayers: Talk over happy times of the day, kindnesses, how God helped—then pray. Begin requests for help: "Help me to remember to cross the street carefully . . . to take turns . . . to help others." Older kindergartners may pray for someone else: "Help the doctor to help Johnny." Begin to distinguish between asking Daddy for toys and asking God to help us take turns. God works through people for physical needs.
CHURCH	Stress happy experiences at church —with other children, —with church workers, —with other classes. Begin association of God and Jesus with the church. Review the prayers prayed and stories heard at church. Visit sanctuary during nonservice time.	Encourage growing enjoyment of child's part in church. Help child to feel that this is his or her church. Find ways to let the child help workers in the church. Help child to be responsible for things: arranging chairs, sharing money gifts for the things we need at church. Continue association of God and Jesus with church.

GRADES 1-3

Continue praise and thanksgiving. Let the child compose his or her own prayers.

Create litany prayers together.

Give opportunities for sentence prayers after discussion of what we are thankful for—don't force the child to pray.

Acknowledge need for forgiveness.

Encourage prayers asking for help, making them more specific than before.

Encourage involvement of the church in the community (shut-ins).

Encourage giving gifts of service for the church: to missionaries, toys for the nursery, etc.

Share with church workers.

Point out that God's house is like our home—we keep it clean. Appreciate the sanctuary and experiences there.

Encourage interest in the ongoing program of the church. Visit the office, see records; see the furnace room, electric meter, cleaning equipment; view order forms for literature. (Say that we give money to help with these things.) Talk with the minister about how the minister uses his or her car, books that are needed, and the fact that he or she has a family. Point out that if the minister is to give his or her days to the church, we must pay to help provide for the minister's family.

GRADES 4-6

Encourage personal and private worship. Provide devotional material.

Help child to appreciate prayers in formal worship.

Study prayers in hymnal for special occasions.

Continue prayer as close relationship with God.

Encourage growth so that this relationship with God is there when child is more independent.

Recognize the developing understanding of the worship service, sacraments, and creeds.

Appreciate all sections of the hymnal.

Begin to appreciate the church symbols; point out that symbols were used to remind people of Bible stories before everyone could read the Bible.

Talk about the heritage of the church to the present day.

Expand knowledge of the church as the church exists around the world.

Stress that there are different churches because there are different beliefs. We all believe in God. Introduce the term "ecumenical."

	NURSERY	KINDERGARTEN
BIBLE	Use simple verses at spontaneous times. Hold the Bible and tell simple stories: children visiting Jesus; Jesus teaching about God; Jesus enjoying nature, Jesus having breakfast with friends; Jesus' babyhood; Mary and Joseph caring for Jesus.	Add stories of Jesus' friends. Tell Old Testament stories that exemplify positive behavior: Miriam's care of her baby brother; Samuel's new coat (his saying "thank you"); Ruth gathering grain and sharing with Naomi; preparing a rooftop room to welcome a visitor. Associate everyday stories with what we learn from the Bible. Use longer, understandable verses. Read verses, using a translation the child can understand. Begin Bible/God association.

Bible Verses for Young Children

Bible words are vehicles to explore meaning in life. We are concerned that our children develop meaning in their lives, not merely memorize words. By paraphrasing some of the verses, we simplify their understanding.

Genesis 1:10	Psalm 96:12b	Matthew 6:31-32
Genesis 1:21	Psalm 100:3	Mark 10:14
Genesis 1:31	Psalm 104:14	Luke 2:10-11
Genesis 8:22	Psalm 104:24	Luke 11:1
Deuteronomy 2:7	Psalm 118:24	John 13:34
Deuteronomy 4:35b	Psalm 145:9	John 21:12
Job 36:31b	Psalm 147:8, 16, 18	1 Corinthians 3:6b
Job 39:11a	Proverbs 6:6, 8	1 Corinthians 3:9
Job 41:31	Proverbs 17:17	1 Corinthians 13:4
Psalm 19:1	Ecclesiastes 3:1	Ephesians 4:15
Psalm 46:10	Ecclesiastes 3:11	Ephesians 4:32
Psalm 92:1	Isaiah 12:2	1 Peter 5:7
Psalm 95:5	Isaiah 14:7	

GRADES 1-3	GRADES 4-6
Make Bible reading a pleasant experience. Be sure passages are simple. Provide opportunities to learn the background from which the Bible comes. Encourage using the Bible in solving our everyday problems. Relate our life to situations in Bible stories: Now we have no roofs to sit on and watch stars—we sit on the deck or in our backyard. We still can enjoy sleeping in tents as in Bible times. Jesus helped the lonely—we help new children in school. Tell about the two parts of the Bible: Old Testament that Joseph read to his family and Jesus enjoyed; New Testament which tells about Jesus and his friends. Tell about the Psalms, the hymnbook of the Bible.	Provide a historical approach to the Bible. Look at the Bible's table of contents; group the books; use the maps. Help child to learn to live by the principles of the Bible. Help child to evaluate own behavior by looking at Jesus' life. Begin to use Old Testament stories showing wrong behavior. Point out that the Old Testament relates growth of Jewish understanding of God and that the New Testament adds to this knowledge. Tell stories about the early church. Show that the New Testament records how Jesus' friends told others about him.

Prepare a Bible with simple verses underlined or highlighted. Place bookmarks in these locations; on the end of each bookmark you may draw a simple picture that relates to the verse. Examples: clouds or sunset—Psalm 19:1; food—Job 36:31b; seashore—Psalm 95:5; cornstalk—Psalm 104:14b; breakfast of fish—John 21:12.

Notes

Chapter 1

[1]Lance Webb, *The Art of Personal Prayer* (Nashville: Abingdon Press, 1962), p. 15.

[2]Frederick Buechner, *The Magnificent Defeat* (New York: The Seabury Press, Inc., 1966), p. 42.

[3]Marilee Zdenek and Marge Champion, *God Is a Verb* (Waco, Tex.: Word, Inc., 1974), p. 32. Used by permission of Word Books, Publisher, Waco, Texas 76796.

Chapter 2

[1]John H. Westerhoff III, *Will Our Children Have Faith?* (New York: The Seabury Press, Inc., 1976), chapter 4. Copyright © 1976 by The Seabury Press, Inc. Used by permission of the publisher.

[2]Donald B. Rogers, *In Praise of Learning* (Nashville: Abingdon Press, 1980), p. 42.

[3]Jean Piaget, *The Moral Judgment of the Child* (New York: The Free Press, a div. of Macmillan Publishing Co., Inc., 1932).

[4]Donald L. Griggs, "God Through the Eyes of a Child," available from the National Teacher Education Program, 7214 East Granada Rd., Scottsdale, AZ 85257.

[5]Keith Miller, *The Becomers* (Waco, Tex: Word, Inc., 1973), p. 52.

Chapter 3

[1]Dorieanne Perrucci, "Paul and Kathie Lee Johnson: A Marriage Whose Music Hits the Charts," *Today's Christian Woman* (Winter-Spring, 1980), p. 11.

[2]Paul Tournier, *A Place for You* (New York: Harper & Row, Publishers, Inc., 1968).

[3]Marilee Zdenek and Marge Champion, *God Is a Verb* (Waco, Tex.: Word, Inc., 1974), p. 32. Used by permission of Word Books, Publisher, Waco, Texas 76796.

[4]Louis Cassels, *The Real Jesus: How He Lived and What He Taught* (New York: Doubleday & Co., Inc., 1968), p. 93.

[5]Mrs. Brooks Hall, shared in *United Methodist Teacher Newsletter*, vol. 4, no. 2 (Summer, 1980).

[6]Donald B. Rogers, *In Praise of Learning* (Nashville: Abingdon Press, 1980), p. 39.

Chapter 4

[1]Cecil Frances Alexander, "All Things Bright and Beautiful," in *The Methodist Hymnal* (Nashville: The Methodist Publishing House, 1964, 1966), p. 34.

[2]Iris V. Cully, *Christian Child Development* (New York: Harper & Row, Publishers, Inc., 1979), p. 28.

[3]Quoted in Lois Bock and Miji Working, *Happiness Is a Family Time Together* (Old Tappan, N.J.: Fleming H. Revell Company, 1975), p. 14.

[4]Frederick Buechner, *The Magnificent Defeat* (New York: The Seabury Press, Inc., 1966), p. 42.

[5]George Herbert, "Let All the World in Every Corner Sing," in *The Methodist Hymnal, op. cit.*, p. 10.

[6]David and Elizabeth Gray, *Children of Joy* (Bradford, Conn.: Readers Press, Inc., 1975), p. 57. Used by permission of the authors.

Chapter 6

[1]John H. Westerhoff III, *Will Our Children Have Faith?* (New York: The Seabury Press, Inc., 1976), p. 36. Copyright © 1976 by The Seabury Press, Inc. Used by permission of the publisher.

[2]Muriel James and Louis Savary, *The Heart of Friendship* (New York: Harper & Row, Publishers, Inc., 1978), p. 13.

Chapter 7

[1]Study by Dr. Eve Allina Lazer of the National Institute of Mental Health in the *New York Times Magazine*, September 22, 1968, p. 190.

[2]Elizabeth L. Reed, *Helping Children with the Mystery of Death* (Nashville: Abingdon Press, 1970), pp. 19-20.

[3]Jo Carr, *Touch the Wind* (Nashville: The Upper Room, 1975), pp. 64-66. Copyright 1975 by The Upper Room, 1908 Grand Avenue, Box 189, Nashville, TN 37202. Used by permission of the Publisher.

[4]Written by Ruth Fahs and quoted in Reed, *op. cit.*, p. 25.

[5]*Ibid.*, p. 33.

[6]Leslie D. Weatherhead, *The Will of God* (Nashville: Abingdon Press, first copyright, Whitmore & Stone, 1944), p. 14. Copyright renewal © 1972 by Leslie D. Weatherhead. Used by permission of the publisher, Abingdon Press.

[7]*Ibid.*, p. 24.

[8]*Ibid.*

[9]Crystal and Ed Zinkiewicz, "Parents: Faith Interpreters," *The Christian Home*, vol. 13, no. 1 (September-November, 1980), p. 7.

Chapter 8

[1]Lance Webb, *The Art of Personal Prayer* (Nashville: Abingdon Press, 1962), p. 9.

[2]*Ibid.*, p. 10.

[3]Albert D. Belden, *The Practice of Prayer* (New York: Harper & Row, Publishers, Inc., 1954), quoted in *ibid.*, pp. 10-11.

Chapter 9

[1]John H. Westerhoff III, *Will Our Children Have Faith?* (New York: The Seabury Press, Inc., 1976), p. 34. Copyright © 1976 by The Seabury Press, Inc. Used by permission of the publisher.

[2]David and Elizabeth Gray, *Children of Joy* (Bradford, Conn.: Readers Press, Inc., 1975), p. 195.

[3]Leslie D. Weatherhead, *The Will of God* (Nashville: Abingdon Press, first copyright, Whitmore & Stone, 1944), pp. 12-14. Copyright renewal © 1972 by Leslie D. Weatherhead. Used by permission of the publisher, Abingdon Press.

Chapter 11

[1]Iris V. Cully, *Christian Child Development* (New York: Harper & Row, Publishers, Inc., 1979), p. 118.

[2]Delia Halverson, "Parents Guide Children to Communion," *The Christian Home*, vol 7, no. 8 (April, 1975), p. 27. Copyright © 1975 by Graded Press.

[3]*Ibid.*, p. 28.

[4]Marilee Zdenek and Marge Champion, *God Is a Verb* (Waco, Tex.: Word, Inc., 1974), p. 32. Used by permission of Word Books, Publisher, Waco, Texas 76796.

Suggested Reading

For the Child

Cassandre, *Making All Things Beautiful*. Valley Forge: Judson Press, 1979. (paperback)

_____, *Life When Jesus Was a Boy*. Valley Forge: Judson Press, 1981. (paperback)

Daves, Michael, *Young Readers Book of Christian Symbolism*. Nashville: Abingdon Press, 1967.

Dotts, Maryann, *When Jesus Was Born*. Nashville: Abingdon Press, 1979.

Goddard, Carrie Lou, *Isn't It a Wonder!* Nashville: Abingdon Press, 1976.

_____, *Jesus*. Nashville: Abingdon Press, 1978.

Gruenberg, Sidonie, *The Wonderful Story of How You Were Born*. Rev. ed. New York: Doubleday & Co., Inc., 1970.

Jones, Mary Alice, *Bible Stories: God at Work with Man*. Nashville: Abingdon Press, 1973.

_____, *Favorite Stories of Jesus*. Skokie, Ill.: Rand McNally & Company, 1981.

Kasuya, Masahiro, *The Way Christmas Came*. Valley Forge: Judson Press, 1973.

Paterson, Katherine, *Bridge to Terabithia*. New York: Harper & Row, Publishers, Inc., 1977. Also available in paperback from Avon Books, 1979.

Peterson, Edward C., and Bullock, Henry M., eds., *Young Reader's Bible*. Nashville: Abingdon Press, 1978.

Pockets (a devotional periodical for elementary children). Available from The Upper Room, 1908 Grand Avenue, P.O. Box 189, Nashville, TN 37202.

Skold, Betty W., *Lord, I Have a Question: Story Devotions for Girls*. Minneapolis: Augsburg Publishing House, 1979. (paperback)

Smith, Doris Buchanan, *A Taste of Blackberries*. New York: Scholastic Book Service, 1976. (paperback; also in hard cover)

Sorenson, Stephen, *Growing Up Isn't Easy, Lord: Story Devotions for Boys*. Minneapolis: Augsburg Publishing House, 1979. (paperback)

Wilt, Joy, *The Nitty-Gritty of Family Life*. Waco, Tex: Word, Inc., 1979. (paperback)

Wolcott, Carolyn M., *I Can See What God Does*. Nashville: Abingdon Press, 1969.

For the Parent

Bock, Lois, and Working, Miji, *Happiness Is a Family Time Together*. Old Tappan, N.J.: Fleming H. Revell Company, 1975.

Carr, Jo, *Touch the Wind*. Nashville: The Upper Room, 1975.

Cully, Iris V., *Christian Child Development*. New York: Harper & Row, Publishers, Inc., 1979.

Gray, David and Elizabeth, *Children of Joy*. Bradford, Conn.: Readers Press, Inc., 1975.

Lewis, Helen Coale, *All About Families the Second Time Around*. Edited by Amy Reynolds. Atlanta: Peachtree Publishers, Ltd., 1980.

Reed, Elizabeth, *Helping Children with the Mystery of Death*. Nashville: Abingdon Press, 1970.

Rowan, Ruth, *Helping Children with Learning Disabilities: In the Home, School, Church and Community*. Nashville: Abingdon Press, 1977.

Weatherhead, Leslie, *The Will of God*. Nashville: Abingdon Press, 1976. (paperback)

Webb, Lance, *The Art of Personal Prayer*. Nashville: Abingdon Press, 1962. Also available in paperback from The Upper Room, 1977.

Westerhoff, John H., III, *Bringing Up Children in the Christian Faith*. Minneapolis: Winston Press, Inc., 1980. (paperback)

_____, *Will Our Children Have Faith?* New York: The Seabury Press, Inc., 1976.

Zinkiewicz, Crystal, *The Anytime Book for Busy Families*. Nashville: The Upper Room, 1979. (paperback)

Index

This index cannot be complete, for each time I reread the manuscript I find something else to add. However, I hope it will help you locate some references in the book to everyday situations as well as concepts you can share spontaneously with your child.